VIRTUOUS REALITY

VIRTUOUS REALITY

How America Surrendered Discussion of Moral Values to Opportunists, Nitwits and Blockheads like William Bennett

Jon Katz

Random House New York

P94 K38 1997

Library of Congress Cataloging-in-Publication Data
Katz, Jon.
Virtuous reality : how America surrendered discussion of moral values to
opportunists, nitwits and blockheads like William Bennett
/ Jon Katz. — 1st ed.
p.   cm.
Includes index.
ISBN 0-679-44913-2
1. Mass media—Moral and ethical aspects.   2. Mass media—
Technological innovations.   I. Title.
P94.K38   1997   302.23—dc20   96-19637

First Edition

FOR ERIC ETHERIDGE

Every Writer Should Be So Lucky

ACKNOWLEDGMENTS

Thanks to Flip Brophy, Ann Godoff, Paula
Span, Jeff Goodell, Jim Oberman, Emma
Span, Tom Snell, Gina Snell, Kristin Kimball,
Martin Beiser, John Battelle, Louis Rossetto,
Jann Wenner, the digital dogs, Rob Gurwitt,
Abbe Don, Marianne Merola, Dr. Rose Oost-
ing, Dr. Susan Buckley, the WELL, David
Weir and the staff of the Netizen, I. F. Stone,
A. J. Liebling, Thomas Paine, Francis Bacon
and John Locke.

CONTENTS

INTRODUCTION

New York Times columnist Bob Herbert was troubled. He'd encountered a poll showing that 60 percent of young Americans were unable to name the president who ordered the nuclear attack on Japan, and that 35 percent didn't know that the first A-bomb was dropped on the Japanese city of Hiroshima. Writing in the familiarly schoolmarmish voice that serious newspapers and broadcasters prefer, Herbert fumed that America has become "a nation of nitwits."

In a different context, insulting and stereotyping an entire country might have provoked outrage. But given current attitudes about media and culture, the idea that we are too stupid to make the "correct" informational choices isn't even controversial. Young people, in particular, are routinely portrayed as ignorant, unacquainted with the basic elements of civilization, unlikely to become good capitalists in the global economy, ill prepared to survive in the adult world. The idea is so often repeated by the news media that it's become a widely accepted article of faith, a central tenet of modern journalism: We represent a superior culture; you'll be sorry for abandoning us. Left to your own devices, you'll read and watch moronic and pointless things and your children will go straight to screen hell.

Intimations of these conflicts go all the way back to the turn of the century, but the start of our cultural civil wars probably dates to 1954, when Dr. Fredric Wertham, a respected psychiatrist, told a congressional committee headed by crime-buster Estes Kefauver that comic books were a major cause of juvenile delinquency, violent crime and deviant sexuality. Wonder Woman promoted lesbianism, warned Wertham, and the relationship between Batman and Robin had "homosexual" overtones. Much worse was just around the corner, had the good doctor but known—the advent of Elvis was mere months away.

A few decades later, we all know the litany: Nobody cares about "real" news anymore. Our standards of literacy, culture and taste have declined past the point of recognition. The tabloids are taking us to hell in an electronic handbasket, obsessed as they are with trashy stories like O.J., Amy Fisher and the Menendez brothers. Our children are mentally deficient, vulnerable to a host of predators lurking out there.

"We are surrounded by a deep and abiding stupidity," Herbert wrote in his op-ed column.

But give him credit for courage: Herbert then sat down, notebook in hand, to venture further than most of his disapproving peers would dare: he encountered the media's reigning cultural antichrist, *Beavis & Butt-head*. The program and its animated antagonists are a merciless spoof of MTV's own adolescent male audience—their belches and bad manners, metalhead musical tastes and general revoltingness.

Herbert's encounter turned out badly. He wrote in his column that *Beavis & Butt-head* was so much worse than anything he could have imagined that he was rendered helpless; he sat before the TV screen in astonishment. "You can't," he wrote, "make notes about *Beavis & Butt-head.*" It's true. You can't. And who but a *New York Times* columnist would even try? Presidents may sputter and fume impotently over the power of *The New York Times,* but the two cartoon creeps from MTV had reduced one of the paper's most prominent writers to bewildered paralysis.

Herbert's denunciation was quickly eclipsed, however, by subsequent alarms and attacks. A few months later, Senator Robert Dole gave his instantly famous "Hollywood" speech, signaling that popular culture would be a central issue in his presidential campaign. "A line has been crossed," he said, "not just of taste, but of human dignity and decency. You know what I mean. I mean *Natural Born Killers. True Romance.* Films that revel in mindless violence and loveless sex." (*Independence Day,* he subsequently declared, passed muster as sufficiently uplifting and patriotic. That it depicted the destruction of America's major cities did not seem to trouble him.)

Dole's speech was recognized as a formal declaration of war. Popular culture long ago stopped being viewed as mere entertainment; it's become a battleground.

The speech coincided, perhaps not accidentally, with a strange but skillful public campaign by two un-likely partners: African-American civil rights activist C. DeLores Tucker and conservative moral guardian William Bennett joined forces to attack Time Warner executives because the company's music division, es-pecially its Interscope subsidiary, presented such con-troversial rap artists as Tupac Shakur and Snoop Doggy Dogg. One Wall Street analyst predicted that Tucker and Bennett's attacks on Warner Music would significantly destabilize the global music business. Shortly afterward, Time Warner announced that Inter-scope was for sale.

There was lots more. In a special report from Har-vard's Neiman Foundation, one of the news media's most prestigious and influential gathering places, Neiman curator William Kovach wrote that radio and television companies, newspapers and newsmagazines had grown comfortable, if not complacent. "As if from nowhere, the great convergence of technology has blown that world apart," he lamented. "Today it seems anyone and everyone, from the phone company to a computer hacker in Oslo, is in the business of making news available."

The entry of "anyone and everyone" into the news business, primarily via cable and computer technology, has shaken the old order right down to its wingtips. For much of this century, news has been controlled by a handful of newspapers, newsmagazines and, more re-cently, broadcast networks. If citizens didn't like what they read or saw, they could write letters of complaint. A few paragraphs might get printed, or the writers might receive an innocuous form letter in return. Period. Consumers had no real access to media.

That has changed, suddenly and radically. Now anybody with a VCR, cable box or computer is a miniature media tycoon, a little Bill Paley. Millions of Americans are faxing, e-mailing and calling voice-mail boxes to sound off on every conceivable political issue. Tens of thousands of idiosyncratic Web sites and home pages have sprung up on the global computer network, the Internet. This is more freedom of the press than journalists conceive of in their worst nightmares.

The different ways in which information now travels seem to be sending much of the country into a kind of cultural nervous breakdown. Americans have an extraordinary love-hate relationship with the rich culture they've created. They buy, watch and read it even as they ban, block and condemn it.

That censorship almost never prevails against the new cultural forms it's designed to protect us from seems to escape our collective memory.

Take the baby boomers who embraced rock and roll, protested the Vietnam War and led the rebellions of the sixties. Now parents themselves—and on edge after years of media warnings about crib death, child snatching, Lyme disease, sexual molestation and other perils, both real and inflated—they're in a near panic about their children's safety. New forms of media are not exciting opportunities to be explored but simply additional dangers to be added to the list.

It seems they were only kidding about the Revolution. On the whole, they are at least as reflexively disapproving as their own parents were, joining forces with William Bennett and other self-serving block-heads to fuss about how tacky and dangerous popular culture is, clucking endlessly about Bart Simpson and *Melrose Place.*

With the vocal support of consummate boomer Bill Clinton, Congress came up with the now notorious Communications Decency Act (CDA), which was quickly and resoundingly overturned by the federal courts, and a technological fix—the "V" (for "violence") computer chip, to be installed in all American television sets so that parents can block programs they don't want children to see. If parents think programming VCRs is tricky, wait till they set out to program control of the hundreds of thousands of hours of TV programming that now beam into households on schedules that vary weekly. The country's biggest provider of online computer services, America Online, has announced "blocking" software to "empower parents" to control what their children see via the Internet. A number of other high-tech firms are marketing software to limit kids' Internet access.

"Americans Despair of Popular Culture," reported a *New York Times* headline in 1995. A survey commissioned by the paper found that far more Americans—21 percent—cited TV as the primary cause of teenage violence than blamed any other factor, including inadequate education, deteriorating family structures or drugs.

Meanwhile, *Time* magazine was publishing the results of a bitterly controversial survey on Internet pornography. *Time*'s cover showed a wild-eyed, terrified child over a "Cyberporn" headline: "A New Study

Shows How Pervasive and Wild It Really Is. Can We Protect Our Kids and Free Speech?" The number of broadcasts, articles and books decrying the dangers of new technology and new media must by now be well into the tens of thousands.

The 1990s are the decade of the Mediaphobe.

The Mediaphobe is frightened and angry. His fear transcends traditional social, cultural and political boundaries. You almost have to admire the unity fear can generate: Civil rights activists join forces with right-wing politicians; ex-hippies take up arms alongside Christian evangelists; a liberal boomer president stands shoulder to shoulder with his conservative challengers. A nation bitterly divided on an array of issues from gun control to Medicaid can unite on this: New media, popular culture, modern information technology—all of it endangers our young, corrodes our civic sphere, decivilizes us all.

The Mediaphobe defines media narrowly. News comes from a thick, sober daily newspaper, read front to back. Or from an evening newscast, with stories presented in order of descending importance. News does not come from *Inside Edition,* Larry King, Ricki Lake or Snoop Doggy Dogg. MTV News doesn't count. Nor does anything on a computer screen.

Yet for all the clucking by the traditional media, Americans both love and embrace the new cultural machinery. VCRs, computers and CD-ROMs are among the best-selling consumer products in American history, approaching portable phones and microwave ovens as ubiquitous fixtures of middle-class life. The computer culture has swiftly metamorphosed from a fringe countercultural movement little known outside its own techie borders to a mainstream information source used by millions of people, inhabited by the elderly, the pet-loving, the religious and the young, as well as nerds, webheads and some of the world's largest corporations.

Notice the apparent contradiction.

Mediaphobia is exactly what it sounds like—not concern about real problems but an anxiety disorder, an increasingly irrational spiral of often unwarranted fears.

This book isn't about high technology or machinery, about which I know very little. It is an argument for more rational ways of comprehending all these changes and figuring out how to feel about them.

This cultural conflict, the endless nyaaah-nyaaahing about old versus new media, is pointless. Old and new media, perpetually at war, have a kind of reflexive arrogance in common: Each camp sees itself as superior to the other.

There is, of course, no good reason for us to have to choose between old and new media. Both are valid and useful in their way, and neither alternative is going to go away. The emergence of new media and broader definitions of culture doesn't mean that newspapers, book publishing or traditional TV newscasts will or should vanish. But we *are* groping for some sort of coherent response to all of the confusing signals we are, sometimes literally, receiving.

My hope is that this book will provide a bit of perspective.

Reader, beware: I do not believe that media are responsible for violence or the degradation of our culture. I think our culture is diverse and exciting, some-times brilliant and creative and sometimes adolescent and vulgar. We need to get past these simpleminded cultural characterizations of good and evil.

Though I'm excited by lots of these changes, new media are not a religion for me. They don't reflect a su-perior civilization, but they do bring us some powerful new political and social ideas, a few bordering on the truly revolutionary. They are a new way to communi-cate and to create relationships and communities. There are good and bad aspects to all this, possibilities that are extraordinary and liberating and others that are discordant, exclusive, invasive and confusing.

A further caveat: I do not believe we are becoming a nation of nitwits, or that our children are in any sense dumber than we were. The ones I know and meet and e-mail every day are plenty smart, very sophisticated about exploring and manipulating complex machinery, and generally more tolerant, curious and open-minded than their parents. The digital revolution was sparked by, and is still led by, the young, for many of whom it is an integral part of their lives. They are never going to give it up. Accusing them of stupidity and obliviousness says more about us than about them. We, not they, will have to change.

Journalism's long war against the culture of the young has proven destructive for both parties. Decades of attacks on comics, rock, rap, TV, cartoons, comput-ers and video games have left traditional journalism with virtually no young readers or viewers. It's too bad that kids can't benefit from the useful things journal-ism offers—not only information but analysis, context, criticism. Meanwhile, the press is committing slow suicide, alienating its future, then scratching its head at its dismal demographics.

For me, the media conflict is personal as well as professional. I was a practicing journalist—at *The Atlantic City Press, The Philadelphia Inquirer, The Washington Post, The Boston Globe, The Baltimore News-American,* the Dallas *Times-Herald,* and finally at CBS News— before I turned media critic and novelist. Like Zorba the Greek's lumber project, my career was a "magnificent catastrophe," but it was a useful window. I watched failure in almost every format: two newspapers that I'd edited subsequently folded; a magazine I helped launch was sold; a TV broadcast I produced collapsed, followed shortly by the network's slow death by takeover. I'm not kidding when I say that this firsthand view of so much disaster has given me an excellent insight into what didn't work about media in the last two decades.

I entered journalism at the end of the time when everyone in the newsroom was named Vince, when reporters worked amid the din of clacking Teletypes, growling copy editors, the hacking coughs of smokers and the bells and roars of smelly giant presses.

I also remember worried executives puzzling over the meaning of VCRs, dismissing cable news as the mad fantasy of Ted Turner and laughing out loud at the idea that people would spend time communicating via computer screens. I recall editors meeting to fret over the defection of suburban readers, noticing that women weren't at home all day anymore, wondering where all the young readers were going.

These are poignant memories of a time that presaged an awful era of sales, mergers, closings, layoffs and a relentless shrinking of creative vision and moral purpose. The news business was never as golden as nostalgia suggests, but it was often great fun, a carnival of vivid characters, a front-row ticket to whatever great events were erupting.

I was run out of journalism after the *CBS Morning News,* whose executive producer I was, collapsed in the late 1980s. I decided there was, shockingly, more security in freelance writing than in working for media conglomerates, and became a media critic. In 1991 my editor at *Rolling Stone* advised that if I wanted to be able to say anything useful about the media, I had to get a new computer and a modem and venture online.

I was lucky enough to join a remarkable community called the WELL, a California-based computer-conferencing system, whose bright, quarrelsome, opinionated, well-informed and generous members took me by the hand electronically and guided me into this new world. I'd come home. In between raging debates about media, religion, politics and the cyberculture, and emotional exchanges about life and death and parenting, there was never a time I asked for help when I didn't get more than I needed.

Sadly, I know very few people in traditional journalism who would say they are having fun or whose papers and broadcast outlets seem to have much energy. But I know lots of people in new media who are having a blast. Including me—I began writing for *Wired,* in addition to more traditional publications, and now host a conference on the Netizen, the political zone of the freewheeling and popular Web site called HotWired.

The experience has left me a media mutant, a critic who lives on the border between two radically different information cultures, appreciating and disliking elements of both. I still love the depth of a good daily newspaper, still appreciate the lively weekly summations of newsmagazines and the longer profiles of their slicker cousins. But I glean most of my news from CNN or e-mail from friends. America Online's hourly news updates alerted me to the latest outrage in the Simpson trial and to the death of Jerry Garcia. I follow hurricane-tracking maps online.

For me, a modem was a gateway to an astonishing new world. I have personally never encountered a pornographer online, but I have talked to spiritualists in Asia, heroic elderly women and men fighting the isolation of the aged via computers, Oxford University historians, black cops struggling to survive amid hostile white colleagues, white cops struggling to deal with the bitter aftermath of having shot someone, a prostitute in Illinois, a descendant of Thomas Paine, a gifted San Francisco transvestite who's been writing a screenplay for two decades, a hacker who sent me an unwanted gift (the unlisted number of an aircraft carrier's flight deck), gay teenagers who aren't alone anymore, the stricken parents of dying children, forgotten friends from elementary school, former colleagues launching new lives in faraway places, and countless readers who tell me off when I write something they don't like, praise me when I write something they do, and suggest ways to improve the ratio. These remarkable people are a stinging rebuke to mediaphobia and the often dumb reporting that fans it.

There is, after all, no reason why Bob Herbert can't just get along with Beavis and Butt-head. It's time for a truce in the media wars. We're simply going to have to live with the fact that we have more information, delivered more rapidly in more diverse forms, than any of us ever imagined, and we're going to have to figure out how to handle it.

Beware, therefore, of windbags and pious souls who presume to know what is moral for you and your family. Stop paying so much attention to the cultural alarmists popping up on talk shows and newspaper op-ed pages. Stay calm. Take a deep breath. This stuff is neither as confusing nor as dangerous as it appears.

Included herein at no extra charge: a media mantra to be recited before your bathroom mirror every morning; to invoke whenever you're horrified by a TV talk-show topic, whenever you're battling with your kids about their latest vitriolic CD or some dopey show on MTV, whenever someone tries to tell you your children are stupider than you were at their age, whenever William Bennett opens his mouth.

THE MEDIA MANTRA

It's not that complicated. I can figure this out. I can make my own decisions about media, values and morality. I don't have to choose between traditional culture and the new media. I can live a happy and fulfilling life even if I never see the World Wide Web.

Whatever they should or shouldn't watch, however much time they spend online, my children are not dumb and they're not in danger from movies, TV shows, music or computers. Many children—especially underclass children—really are suffering from horrific violence, and they need more and better parenting, better schools, fewer guns and drugs and lots of job opportunities. If I'm so worried about kids, I will help them.

If I really want to protect my own children, I will make sure they have more, not less, access to this new cultural and technological world. I won't ever call them stupid for watching things I don't like. I don't have to be at war with them. I can work out a social contract with my children that protects them, guides them through their new culture and brings peace and rationality to our house.

Amen.

As for me, I can be e-mailed at JDKatz@aol.com

VIRTUOUS REALITY

MEDIA a'la CARTE

NEWSPAPER 1.23
RADIO 2.95
TELEVISION 3.45
COMPUTER ...... OUT

ADD CHEESE TO ANY
OF THE ABOVE ITEMS
FOR ONLY $0.45

MEDIA CARTE

KRQR

CALIFORNIA
TD 7804

106 KMEL

415 863 4149

Chapter 1

A BRIEF AND IDIOSYNCRATIC HISTORY

This is neither our first information revolution, nor our last. It's not the first time our values have seemed in danger of being turned upside down. At the end of the twelfth century, monks from all over Europe came to Paris to laboriously hand-produce, for the first time, huge numbers of single-volume portable Bibles. They were the first best-sellers, distributed throughout Christendom, and the impact was explosive. No other information entity had ever been distributed so broadly. No ideology had ever been transmitted so quickly or widely. Culture, religion, politics and literacy were never the same.

The printing press, the telegraph, the telephone, radio, TV, the computer—new kinds of information-delivery systems break over us in great, dislocating waves, each wave bearing along its own zealots, prophets, advocates and critics.

It's easy to miss the distinct pattern that flows from the Bibles the Paris scribes laboriously copied to the modem the contemporary teen uses to shake hands with the rest of the world. The media, the contemporary institution most responsible for clarifying these kinds of changes and putting them in useful perspective, rarely do: journalists are too preoccupied with daily deadlines and too muffled by convention. But from the Bible to the PC, we have been moving toward a world that links us in ways that were never before possible.

This progression has never been greeted with unequivocal enthusiasm. Each step forward seems to take something away. We appreciate the convenience of the phone, but we lose privacy and solitude. We enjoy TV, but we don't like all the things we see on it. We learn to rely on computers, but we fear they are isolating us or exposing our children to the whole scary world. But each of these milestones marks movement, however lurching, in the same direction: connecting us.

Though the information revolution in twelfth-century Paris may have come as more of a shock— we've seen a few; we're jaded—the one we're in the midst of now is a whopper. Access to and distribution of information is changing daily. Millions of people are speaking to one another in ways that were unimaginable just a few years ago, forming communities, gaining access to the archives of the world. Individuals with the will, resources and time are hooking up to vast global networks that transmit messages, text and graphics instantly.

Once again, our ideas of community, culture, literacy and politics are under assault; once again, there is an outcry that the price is too high, that our kids are zombies, that we will become a nation of hermits, that vivid imagery can turn us violent—that our civilization is being undermined.

DAYS OF YORE

America's first journalists were passionate debaters and social advocates. Thomas Paine, the father of outspoken democratic journalism, came to the colonies from England, wrote the pamphlet *Common Sense* (the country's first best-seller) and ignited a firestorm. He believed journalism should be a force for social change and attacked monarchies, organized religion, slavery. He faced imprisonment or death in both England and France. He refused most royalties, believing his work would reach more people if it was cheap to buy. He died in poverty.

He bears no relationship of any sort to most of his professional descendants and would surely fall to his knees and weep at the sight of the well-paid, self-righteous, blow-dried crowd that gathers several times a day in the White House Briefing Room, demanding to be fed.

The journalism Paine practiced was open to anybody, not just a few members of an arrogant elite. It circulated via pamphlets, handbills, posters. An ill-educated but opinionated farmer in New England, for instance, published *The Reformer* to argue about agricultural policy.

This sort of medium was doomed from the first, as even Paine suspected. America's capitalistic and corporate ethic is relentless. As the machinery of media became more expensive, fewer citizens could afford to use it. Individuals were steadily driven out, forced to be consumers, not participants. Media became corporatized over the next two centuries, while competition dwindled, along with a sense of passion and moral purpose. No newspaper in America would hire the outspoken Thomas Paine today.

RISE OF THE WIDGET MAKERS

At the beginning of the nineteenth century, newspapers were blatantly partisan, affiliated with political parties and their leaders. They identified themselves quite openly as favoring one point of view or another; their mission was to beat the drums for their party and its platform. Papers raged furiously at one another and at opposing politicians.

But advances in printing technology like the rotary press gradually made papers richer, more powerful, more broadly circulating, and individual voices receded into the background. Modern media executives have only refined the lessons learned by mid-nineteenth-century publishers—the blander you are, the more people you can reach, the more advertisers you can attract. To be outspoken is to offend; to offend is to alienate consumers; to alienate consumers is to earn less money.

Publishers named this sanitized view of the role of the press "objectivity" and made it journalism's primary moral imperative. To be "objective" was to be professional, detached.

The Civil War furthered the idea by introducing the "correspondent"—the reporter who, through his paper, provides citizens far from the scene with an honest, balanced view of a major story. For readers of that era, not only was the future of their country at stake, but their fathers, brothers and sons were fighting and dying in faraway battles. The information that correspondents sent back was literally life or death; it was supposed to be dependable.

Ever since, the ethos of journalism has been for reporters to go where we couldn't go, see what we couldn't see and tell us about it. In the early days of the press, there was almost no distinction between citizens and journalists: We were them. As the country grew and the stories became bigger, more complex and more distant, the idea of the professional reporter as surrogate grew as well. Since we couldn't get to the aftermath of hurricanes, riots, train wrecks or building collapses, reporters became our eyes and ears. It was the beginning of the modern media's most central role in our lives—they were the observers.

They particularly played this role in Washington, still physically remote from most of the country. Since citizens could rarely read legislation for themselves or meet congresspeople or presidents, the press met them for us and acted—at least in theory—on our behalf.

The function made the press enormously powerful, not in Paine's advocacy role but in a different role—as gatekeeper. If the press didn't put an issue on the national agenda, it didn't get there. Increasingly, individual, non-journalistic voices receded. Citizens stopped participating in journalism, which was becoming a quasiprofession, and were reduced instead to writing letters to editors.

It was the start of what has become a widening estrangement. The press and the public have been on different paths ever since, each pursuing its own goals, each steadily losing touch with what the other is about.

Almost all major journalistic outlets are now part of conglomerates—newspaper chains, regional companies with print and broadcast properties, vast megacorporations like Gannett, Time Warner–Turner, Fox, Westinghouse, Disney–Capital Cities. However they vary in editorial independence, moral courage or commitment to journalistic values, collectively such companies are Tom Paine's and Thomas Jefferson's worst nightmare—mass media dominated not by passionate, informed, individual citizens, but by wealthy corporate entities loyal primarily to stockholders and Wall Street analysts. As an inevitable consequence of the mass-marketing its practitioners are now forced to practice, journalism has become militantly moderate on most issues, struggling to offend the fewest.

It has become exclusive, relegating most individuals to the role of passive consumers. It has ghettoized commentary, restricting opinions to editorial and op-ed pages. Journalism seems less concerned about provoking the powerful than about snuggling up to political insiders, raking in fat speaking fees and book advances, getting into the hot parties. It has worked havoc upon national politics, subjecting candidates and office holders to unending inquisitions about their personal lives. It is addicted to controversy, ceaselessly relaying arguments rather than helping us resolve problems.

The evolution from opinions to objectivity, from individual control to monopolized corporate voices, from radical outsider to moderate insider, has left the press less and less able to confront the truth about issues like crime, race, gender or criminal justice. As we grapple with the many issues raised by the O. J. Simpson trial, for instance, we can see how dearly we are paying for its failure of nerve and loss of moral purpose. We are shocked at the divisions the Simpson verdict revealed. We are amazed when hundreds of thousands of black men follow Louis Farrakhan to Washington.

The only difference between widget makers and newspaper publishers now is that while both hustle widgets, one pretends he's following in the footsteps of Thomas Jefferson.

Increasingly, though, this modern journalistic structure has been engulfed by new competitors. By nerds with computers. By online bulletin boards encroaching on news functions. By brash filmmakers taking on race, history and social issues. By radio talk-show hosts whose ferociously outspoken opinions make newspaper op-ed pages seem even grayer than they are. By TV writers reinventing drama in prime time. By cable channels offering true diversity: music videos, old documentaries, political satire. By talk, tabloid and reality shows pursuing compelling though sometimes irresponsible agendas. And by the World Wide Web, a network of linked Internet sites touching off one of the great creative explosions of modern culture.

HNOCHED OFF OUR PINS

We are slack-jawed at all of these changes in the way information moves around, in the freewheeling content of culture, in our children's access to this complicated world. And at the heated conflict of values that media and culture have touched off in America.

The few institutions that used to decide what was important have been rudely elbowed aside by ferociously diverse and outspoken new information media. To the horror of our traditional press, what matters most in this strange new world is not what editors and producers tell us is important but what we ourselves decide is interesting.

We might as well tear up the cultural scorecard and start over. Rules are shattered, meanings inverted. The gatekeepers are on the run, panicked and sounding the alarm. Kids who used to choose between comic books and sitcoms manipulate vast little communications empires that link them to the whole planet.

No one can even define what we used to call "news." In one of our biggest stories in years, the O. J. Simpson trial, Geraldo Rivera and the *National Enquirer* provided serious reporting and commentary while some of our most "serious" journalists seemed paralyzed, unable to tell us what was really happening, setting us up for the Great Shocker that ended the trial.

Oliver Stone, now that he's done with Vietnam and JFK's assassination, is as likely to be reinterpreting Nixon as *The Washington Post* is. Comedy Central is as likely to offer gavel-to-gavel coverage of presidential nominating conventions as CBS News. And presidential candidates are just as likely to pop up on *Oprah* as on *World News Tonight*. More likely, in fact, if the candidates are reading their own demographic studies and opinion polls. Meanwhile, MTV News does what newspapers have failed to do for decades—arouses hundreds of thousands of young voters and sends them to the polls.

All of this has sent serious journalism and its adherents into a prolonged nervous breakdown. The mainstream press used to have a monopoly on serious stuff and serious news consumers. Now everybody has to share.

And not everybody is happy about it, as usual.

Opportunistic politicians are sounding alarms. Hype-addicted journalists are frightening us. Teachers aren't quite sure what to teach. Parents are anxious and twitchy. And the gap between those who are adept with these new machines and those who can't afford them is unnerving. The machinery itself is never what's important. What most of us care most about is not how information is transmitted but the values it supplants, reinforces or alters. Is technology a good witch or a bad witch? Are our children lucky or endangered? Has political discourse collapsed or is it being reborn? Does all this new cultural expression reflect violence or create it? Make us smarter or dumber? More communitarian or more isolated?

Amidst the technohype about computers, modems, the Internet, the Web, PCTVs, band width and CD-ROMs, what are we supposed to make of it all? Given the confusion, it's understandable that so many otherwise thoughtful people want the unfamiliar and unsettling new media to Just Go Away.

But the notion that we must choose between the old and the new, between one information culture and another, is false. We face complicated choices, but not as complicated as we are being led to believe. We can come to see that the decisions we must make about information and culture are not altogether different from those we confront in any supermarket, where we are presented with so much attractive packaging, so much waxed and polished produce, so much more of everything than we need or can eat. We can learn to pick a bit of this and a little of that, to see behind the hype, to make our own decisions.

Chapter 2

ENTER THE MEDIAPHOBE—STAGE RIGHT AND STAGE LEFT

The Mediaphobe is everywhere: in Congress, on campus, at the pediatrician's office and the supermarket checkout counter. Wherever parents gather to watch their kids play soccer or to hold PTA meetings, there dwells the Mediaphobe.

He's had a couple of great years lately, perhaps his strongest since the early denunciations of rock and roll. He persuaded Congress to pass a law banning indecency on the Internet (promptly overturned) and mandating the V-chip. He got a number of movies and TV shows blamed for acts of copycat violence. He forced a big media conglomerate to sell off its gangsta rap music division. He is responsible for a presidential candidate's fulminations against Hollywood. He pressured advertisers to boycott trashy TV talk shows.

But the mediaphobes are hoping for more. They're still anxious and outraged, still clucking over violent cartoons, rolling their eyes over provocative lyrics and graphic videos. You can hear them swapping their horror stories and survival stratagems: *She doesn't read anymore. He ought to be doing his homework first. I won't let them watch all that junk; they just turn into zombies. My phone bill is going through the roof. How do you know what they're doing up there? They could be talking to anybody.*

Living rooms, cineplexes and kids' bedrooms have become cultural battlegrounds. *Turn off the TV. Get off the computer. We're going to block MTV, drop AOL, cancel the cable.*

American Online, more and more aping the behavior of the traditional media organizations it once tried to supplant, proudly announced new blocking software to make it simpler to control the young online as well. Parents can put off-limits any content they fear, disagree with, feel vaguely uncomfortable about. Call it cultural sanitizing. "Parents will be able to block all but Kids Only, the area of the service with content targeted and programmed specifically for children," an AOL press release proclaimed. The idea, it said, was to "empower parents with the appropriate tools" to restrict access.

Other software manufacturers are developing even more sophisticated software to permit parents to block any Internet topic, discussion or file containing words, language or subjects the parents find offensive.

The Mediaphobe was surely happy to hear the good news about blocking software. Such mechanisms are generally unnecessary and, given the technical skills and ingenuity of the young, highly unlikely to work for

very long—but so what? Increasingly flummoxed by all the choices facing his offspring, the Mediaphobe wants to ban more and more things these days. He feels the ground shifting, his fixed points collapsing. Newspapers are in trouble, network TV news has been marginalized, the Washington pundits grow increasingly useless.

The Mediaphobe frequently couches his panic in terms of dangers to others, particularly children. But he's really afraid for himself, of what he doesn't know or is too lazy or intimidated to learn, of the scary new world on the other side of the screen.

NO WONDER

You can't blame the Mediaphobe for being afraid. Many of his political representatives and his media outlets are telling him he should be. In its "Cyberporn" cover story published in June 1995, *Time* magazine suggested the Internet was swarming with pornographers and peddlers of bestiality. The FBI raided alleged child pornographers across the country in a sting operation set up via America Online. Senator James Exon—with the help of Gary Hart's ex-mistress Donna Rice Hughes—pushed a noxious bill through Congress prohibiting "lewd, lascivious, filthy or indecent" imagery in cyberspace. Meanwhile, the press reported that bomb-making tips and hate literature were also being downloaded by teenaged psychotics. Writing in *Newsweek,* an American University professor of literature even predicted the death of the apostrophe, "because reading is dead." Professor Charles R. Larson continued, "Soon, no one will be certain about grammatical usage anyway. Computers will come without an apostrophe key. Why bother about errors on the Internet?"

Books warned that computers were unleashing a whole host of evils. Social historian Kirkpatrick Sale wrote, in *Rebels Against the Future,* that technology was destroying the planet. Technophobe Jeremy Rifkin argued, in *The End of Work,* that within the coming century, technology will render all workers superfluous. Movies like *The Net* and *Virtuosity* suggest a new technoworld that invades our privacy, destroys our freedom or just plain slaughters us. Our country's media and civic intellectuals are in vocal despair.

In fact, new media practitioners *are* often hostile to enormous concentrations of power in few hands. They *do* have little use for conventions like objectivity. They like being able to express their opinions as well as read columnists' and editorialists'.

These enormous differences in values are, as William Kovach of the Nieman Foundation suggests, at the heart of the tension between the new and old information cultures. They help explain why the relentlessly hostile and alarmist coverage of the new information culture and technologies has given rise to epidemic mediaphobia.

STRANGE BEDFELL—UH—STRANGE ALLIES

It's practically an American tradition for certain members of the clergy and community leaders to be at odds with free speech and freewheeling culture, denouncing prostitution, pornography, liquor and tobacco, even forms of singing and dancing.

But mediaphobia is no longer limited to the religious right or to your run-of-the-mill concerned clergy. Nor is it limited to political conservatives, like Bennett and Dole, who use the issue to sell fat hardcovers or rally voter support.

The mediaphobes have assembled a remarkably diverse coalition. To the mix of religious and cultural conservatives have been added the once-rebellious boomers, the children of the sixties whose plunge into parenting has pushed them into the culture wars. Affluent, educated boomers are astonishingly fearful parents. Taking cues—and much of their information— from lazy news media, they have adopted the serious social problems that are far more likely to threaten the poor—crime, AIDS, cripplingly bad education—and transferred their anxiety about them to their own children, who are continually warned about everything from sex to strangers.

These groups agree on little except how dangerous new media are; they share a common desire for ways to control or discourage them. A *New York Times* columnist is as likely to decry new media and culture as a fundamentalist minister; a boomer parent takes the same cultural point of view as censor-happy blockheads like Charlton Heston; a feminist academic may attack music videos as happily as a right-wing Republican. In Berkeley, a group of college students gathered to kick and smash television sets as an act of "therapy for the victims of technology."

The astonishing breadth of concern suggests that a

deeper chord has been touched than worry over violence or explicit sexual imagery can explain. What's at stake appears to be something more basic: the sense that we are in command of our children and our immediate worlds. Mediaphobes mostly fear that they are losing control. And they're probably right.

They seem to think that rather than learning and teaching about the new world, they can stave it off by branding it satanic, sort of like desperately holding up a sprig of wolfsbane—or a V-chip—against a vampire. As anybody who goes to the movies knows, the monster is only briefly deterred; he is too powerful to be so easily vanquished.

Mediaphobes are afraid, though they can't say precisely what they're afraid of. They are quick to denounce censorship but quicker to censor. They pride themselves on their open-mindedness but seem terrified of new ideas and change. They want their children to thrive in the larger world but block access to the very tools and culture they'll need to learn about in order to do that. They either don't know or have forgotten that emerging culture has always seemed dangerous to the entrenched.

The Mediaphobe rarely manages to block the right thing. Instead of getting rid of the guns that kill people, he tries to bump off the cartoons and rap records that don't. Instead of altering the circumstances that generate violence, he wants a V-chip in his TV so he doesn't have to see pictures of it anymore.

History is full of people with similar impulses. If the past tells us anything, it's that the curious and the innovative ultimately prevail. Put your money on the kids.

Chapter 3

KING OF THE MEDIAPHOBES

If you've ever wondered why politicians and public institutions have so little credibility or moral authority and why the young increasingly want nothing to do with either, take a few minutes to consider the spectacularly American phenomenon that is William Bennett. This is a man whose life will make your jaw drop.

Just a few years ago, Bennett was near the top of our governmental hierarchy, serving George Bush as the nation's first drug czar, charged with stemming the epidemic of drug abuse. He'd previously served as Ronald Reagan's secretary of education, responsible for shoring up the country's failing public education system.

But Bennett didn't labor long in those bleak vineyards. No fool, he quickly fled to a more lucrative and ultimately more powerful position: First Warrior in the battle over cultural values.

Less benevolent and forgiving societies used to send people into exile—or worse—for messing up on the scale Bennett has. Drug policy and deteriorating schools are acknowledged to be two of the more tragic public policy disasters in modern memory. In other cultures—Japan's comes to mind—Bennett might have left the public arena in shame or thrown himself upon an ancestral blade.

But in shame-free America, extreme failure in the pursuit of self-righteousness is no vice. In fact, it's a marketing opportunity. Far from brooding quietly over the untamed drug epidemic or failing schools, Bennett has taught us all a thing or two about gall and redemption, inspiring everyone who blunders spectacularly and wonders if there's life beyond.

Bennett now serves as our reigning, if self-appointed, national virtues czar, the scourge of popular culture, rescuer of our brain-fried young, chief ideologist for the many Americans who think the new media and pop culture are taking us straight to hell.

Though he has concentrated so far on rap and talk shows and the general absence of virtue in popular culture, believe this: Bennett is just warming up. Wait till he gets a look at the live conversation rooms of AOL's Teen Chat or some of the Web's spicier satanic newsgroups.

Bennett is the big mouth in the mediaphobia movement, the guy with the weightiest Rolodex. He nibbles on the ears of presidential wanna-bes, press pundits and members of Congress. He sells zillions of books, humbles the biggest corporations, and can put every talk-show producer in the country on the defensive with a single press conference.

Bennett may be at a loss to know how to stop drugs, improve schools or end the slaughter of kids on city streets, but he has an unerring sense of the yearning many adults have for simple definitions of right and wrong to preach to their kids. *The Book of Virtues,* his 1992 anthology, earned him an estimated five million dollars in three years. Not bad for a book he didn't write. Except for the introduction and some moral asides, all the poems, fables and folktales within are other authors' work, many of them altered to be less provocative or controversial. Want him to come talk to your Sunday school class? He charges forty thousand dollars per lecture.

Bennett's reemergence is all the more remarkable, given the consensus that he has lots of smarts but all the charm and compassion of a chain-link fence. Bennett, wrote Michael Kelly in a frank *New Yorker* profile, is, "inarguably, an opportunist. He is also something of a bully, an overbearing ex-jock who traffics in confrontation and intimidation rather than reasoned discourse. He is rude. . . . He is a Barnumesque sensationalist, a light-fingered popularizer of others' ideas, and an unregenerate middlebrow. . . . He is a self-promoting, self-important sermonizer."

Heads-up families might want to keep such a man as far away from their kids as possible. Instead, anxious parents, manipulable journalists and greedy publishers have legitimized him as a dispenser of moral parables, our national arbiter of decency. Fear of talk shows, gangsta rap and online grunge are already so widespread that no price seems too high to pay to someone peddling talismans that can ward off the modern world.

So Bennett functions as a dealer, selling cultural crack to mediaphobes at thirty dollars a hardcover pop. Like many successful dealers, he doesn't bother to manufacture the stuff himself. He's a distributor.

The Book of Virtues is, in some ways, a bargain. At 831 pages (and about five pounds), *Virtues* can stop all but the heaviest doors. Dropped on a burglar, it would prove disabling if not lethal. But as to its practical use moralitywise, it's a bit thin.

The book, says Bennett in his brief introduction, is intended to aid in the education of the young: "Moral education—the training of heart and mind toward the good—involves many things. It involves rules and precepts—the do's and don'ts of life with others—as well as explicit instruction, exhortation, and training." Accordingly, Bennett sprinkles in his own exhortations, usually one- or two-line morals. Children beleaguered by guns, drugs, bad schools, or abusive parents can seek comfort in the likes of "The Funeral Oration of Pericles," by Thucydides, or "The Song of the Bee," by Marian Douglas.

> Buzz! Buzz! Buzz!
> This is the song of the bee.
> His legs are of yellow;
> A jolly, good fellow,
> And yet a great worker is he.

In case they miss the point, Bennett supplies the moral: "God seems to have created bees to inspire us toward industry."

Bennett's describes his book as a "how-to book for moral literacy." It reads like the hearty homilies

spouted by Homer Simpson's painfully earnest neighbor Ned Flanders ("Okily-dokily, neighbor"). Nevertheless, it's become a trilogy, followed by *The Children's
Book of Virtues* (twenty dollars) and *The Moral Compass* (thirty dollars). Just eighty dollars buys scores of
stories that, if nothing else, keep kids off the streets by
boring them into insensate numbness.

Real moral: You don't actually have to produce
anything; you can make a lot of money off other
people's work.

Like many whose difficult undertaking it is to improve the rest of us, Bennett professes a reluctance to
take on this task. It's the demands of his adoring public
that compel him: "Originally, I had not intended to put
together a second collection of moral stories, and
agreed to do so only at the urging of readers who loved
the material they found in *The Book of Virtues* and
wrote to ask for more."

The Moral Compass presents the same virtues but in
a different marketing context, "the stages of a life's jour-
ney." As in the reprinted poem "Twenty Froggies," by
George Cooper, whose first two stanzas are as follows:

> Twenty froggies went to school
> Down beside a rushy pool,
> Twenty little coats of green,
> Twenty vests all white and clean.

> "We must be in time," said they,
> "First we study, then we play;
> That is how we keep the rule,
> When we froggies go to school."

Inevitably in such disciplined froggies, they go on to prosper as bullfrogs.

> Polished to a high degree,
> As each froggie ought to be.
> Now they sit on other logs,
> Teaching other little frogs.

The moral in "Twenty Froggies"? "A great event in every young life is that long-awaited first day of going to school. This little poem helps us get ready."

Moral: There's big bucks in patronizing the young.

A personal note: Striving to be fair-minded, I took "Twenty Froggies" to an elementary school in the town where I live.

As I approached a half dozen third graders, a teacher loomed immediately and asked me to leave. "But it's William Bennett's book," I said, and she smiled and backed off as if I had waved the proper hall pass. "Oh, we have some of those books," she said. "We've been reading them to the kids for a year or so. Aren't they great?" She gave me permission to read "Twenty Froggies" under her watchful eye.

So I read. The kids looked at one another and began giggling. "These frogs couldn't wait to start school?" Peter snorted. His friends laughed uproariously. The very notion made their day.

At a local middle school, I approached a couple of boys who looked about twelve and showed them "Waukeka's Eagle," a tale of how the "Indian Boy

Waukeka" found a young eagle with a broken wing and nursed it back to health.

"You paid thirty dollars for that?" one kid asked, shaking his head.

His friend leafed through the pages. "Better than math homework." He leafed some more. "Maybe not."

As for my own teenage daughter, I let her browse through a couple of stories and asked if she wanted me to read them to her. "You'll have to kill me first," she said.

BUCKLING TO BULLIES

It wouldn't matter so much if Bennett were just the latest in a long line of hustlers hawking potions to prolong life, shrink tumors and cure impotence. But his predecessors didn't advise office-holders and -seekers or dream of taking themselves or their wares so seriously. Bennett takes himself very seriously, and is taken seriously by others.

He is a political heavyweight, some say even a possible presidential candidate. He advises key Republicans and helps shape the party's ideology and philosophy. Because of his political muscle in Congress and in government agencies, there is always implicit in his bullying the idea that regulation or legislation will follow if the benighted don't take his advice.

Aside from his best-sellers, he helped mastermind a major, if totally illusory, victory against the megacompanies who control much of media and popular culture. Joining with African-American political activist C. DeLores Tucker and with Barbara Wyatt, head of the Parents' Music Resource Center (the protect-our-kids-from-rock-lyrics group Tipper Gore launched), he humbled giant Time Warner, which subsequently sold its stake in Interscope Records. Interscope produced some of the most controversial and successful hard-core rap artists in America.

Bennett and Tucker's assault was a classic and will help chart the way for any group of people who find one or another segment of culture offensive. The two complemented each other perfectly—the Democratic activist accusing Time Warner of "training black people to be not fit for a decent society" and the archconservative Republican media manipulator screaming about morals and providing supporting fire in the form of stories, columns and TV features. Time Warner couldn't dismiss complaints about rap as either the rantings of the far right or the reflexive twitching of the politically correct.

Using carefully plotted protests at stockholder meetings, dramatic face-to-face confrontations with Time Warner executives, ads in newspapers and magazines and the eagerness of the traditional news media to attack any culture that isn't Disneyfied, Bennett has kept the pressure on.

Large media conglomerates are feared for their enormous power, but as the confrontation with Time Warner demonstrated, they are corporate chicken-hearts, extremely vulnerable to outside pressure and unpleasant public relations. Time Warner has a history of buckling under. It folded under an earlier, similar protest against Ice-T's song "Cop Killer," canceling Ice-T's contract. Similarly, Viacom caved in to unproved—but widely reported—allegations that *Beavis & Butt-head* promoted copycat violence, dropping the animated show from its early MTV time slot and censoring its language and content.

Modern media companies are no longer run by powerful individuals willing to take heat for their decisions, but by conglomerates of corporate lawyers, Wall Street analysts, directors and powerful stockholders—all of whom dread controversy and legal difficulties because negative publicity can adversely affect stock prices and mergers, or even call down federal regulation.

These companies need little incentive to jettison an artist or run from fights, especially those as skillfully orchestrated as Bennett's. Giant MCA subsequently bought Time Warner's stake in Interscope; we'll see whether it tolerates messages like Tupac Shakur's better.

It doesn't take a civil libertarian to foresee the possible consequences. If companies like Viacom, Disney, MCA and Time Warner control the acquisition, production and distribution of much of American popular culture, and if they dump artists and producers who become subject to political attack, then everything we see will end up looking as bland and safe as *The Reader's Digest*. Or *The Book of Virtues*. Which seems to be Bennett's big idea.

After Time Warner's capitulation, he once again generated enormous publicity by attacking daytime TV talk shows as celebrating the "underside" of American life. He warned producers to clean up or face viewer boycotts. The programs, filled with confessions, betrayals and confrontations, were increasingly popular among kids home from school.

In May 1996, he went on the attack again. Joined by Tucker and two Democratic senators, he renewed his assault on rap as "a great big cultural cancer" and announced a radio-and-petition campaign.

You can take to the bank the notion that rampaging Bennettism will soon focus on other new media, especially digital culture. The Net is the complete antithesis of the cultural notions advanced in Bennett's tomes. Celebrating individual expression, not conforming to cultural tradition, the Net is often irreverent, loud, devoted to the ferocious exchange of ideas and information. A small but vigorous part of it is explicitly sexual. It is frequently profane, idiosyncratic, rebellious and combative.

Much of America already believes that the Internet is riddled with pornographers, thieves and hackers. Most newsgroups and Web sites are, by design, completely uncensored. If daytime talk shows, which do little demonstrable damage beyond providing tasteless entertainment, provoke so much controversy, it's not much of a stretch to imagine Bennett and his pious legions of mediaphobes next demanding restrictions on the Net.

BLAME IT ON THE BOSSA NOVA

There's so much that's dumb and simpleminded about Bennett's notions of virtue that it's astonishing to see them embraced and disseminated so enthusiastically through the mass media. It's hard to think of more irrelevant exercises for hard-pressed contemporary children, or a bigger waste of their parents' hard-earned money, than these bloated collections of clichés. Yet Bennett now resides in the computerized Rolodex of every reporter looking for a quote on the state of the nation's moral health. *"The Book of Virtues* ought to be distributed, like an owner's manual, to new parents leaving the hospital," gushed *Time.*

Bennett's profilers have gone to great pains to point out that he is a faithful husband, attentive father and regular churchgoer—as if those traits qualify him to tell the rest of us what's right or wrong. What Thomas Merton had to say about such scolds may be more pertinent. Merton, a Trappist monk who wrote widely on values and spirituality, made a point of declaring his uncertainty and doubt, not only about his own life but about the behavior of others.

"It sometimes happens," he wrote in *Seeds of Reflection,* "that men who preach most vehemently about evil and the punishment of evil, so that they seem to have practically nothing else on their minds except sin, are really unconscious haters of other men. They think the world does not appreciate them, and this is their way of getting even."

Definitions of morality are personal and can vary widely. But the real moral tale, of course, is that of Bennett himself.

During the mid-sixties, he was, by his own accounts, involved with "left-wing" stuff, especially civil rights. He studied philosophy at the University of Texas, where he fell into the hands of John Silber—now the deeply conservative president of Boston University, then so attuned to the Left that he advised the school's SDS chapter. Bennett taught philosophy, then ran a humanities think tank in North Carolina until Ronald Reagan picked him to head the National Endowment for the Humanities in 1981. There, his particular brand of attack conservatism caught the imagination of the Right, the media and the GOP. One of his first official acts was to denounce a TV documentary on the Nicaraguan revolution, made with an NEH grant, as "unabashed socialist-realism propaganda."

Reagan appointed Bennett secretary of education in 1985. He was named national director of drug-control policy by George Bush four years later but quit after only twenty months, claiming to be tired from three successive government jobs.

Unfortunately, he didn't rest. He switched to marketing and media, selling nostrums that would calm the panic of a middle class drowning in all this New Stuff.

Bennett claimed great success in his "war on drugs," but few knowledgeable drug-policy scholars agreed. During his tenure, the number of murders rose to more than twenty-three thousand per year, the bloodiest record for civilians in the nation's history; police said drug-related violence was the major factor. Bennett claimed the rising drug-homicide rate was a sign that the effort to stop illegal drug traffic was succeeding, because dealers were killing one another in an effort to attract dwindling numbers of customers. Under questioning, he conceded that this was "perhaps counterintuitive."

Bennett had three ideas as drug czar: more cops, more arrests, tougher sentences. As a result, the United States' imprisonment rate by 1991 was higher than South Africa's or the former Soviet Union's. Former New York City police commissioner Patrick V. Murphy was among the skeptics: "When all those huge drug sweeps in '89 and '90 were over, most of the chiefs said we didn't accomplish anything."

In fact, federal officials report that illicit drug use by teenagers increased significantly in the next year or two, driven by a dramatic rise in the use of marijuana and increases in the use of stimulants, LSD and inhalants. Bennett immediately blamed the Clinton administration.

Bennett's record as education secretary was, if possible, even worse. In his first press conference 1985, he called college students "beach bums" who "ought to give up their stereos to pay tuition instead of expecting government aid."

As Bennett left the Bush administration in 1990, President Bush called a meeting of the nation's governors to talk about a string of bleak reports about American education. The country's high schools were graduating seven hundred thousand functionally illiterate students a year. An equal number dropped out before graduation. Forty-five percent of high school seniors in one urban area couldn't find the United States on a world map.

The day Bennett left the Education Department, College Board officials released results showing combined math-verbal SAT scores for U.S. high school students had dropped for the first time in eight years. Bennett blamed "the school establishment."

Moral: Take the money and run. And never accept responsibility if you can blame somebody else.

PETER RABBIT AND RICKI LAKE

We all know Bennett's thirty-dollar placebos are useless, that people buy them because they make them feel better, that they represent not the world we live in but the one some of us wish we did. We also know that the kids most in need of hope and uplifting will never get near a William Bennett hardcover and would run screaming in horror if they did. The joke is on us, but it isn't funny—our children will have to make their way through the new culture and technology as best they can, apparently with little sane help from us.

Our guardians are so busy condemning children's culture that they forget it is, almost by definition, rebellious, offensive, different from ours. That is often the whole point of youth culture—to differentiate one generation from another. We're not supposed to like it.

Rap lyrics can seem sexist, violent and crude or the natural reflection of a country filled with guns, drugs, racial divisions, overwhelmed schools and broken families. Talk shows can be "freak shows" to someone like Bennett or logical mirrors of the social, gender and class upheavals the guests experience daily and share through their ritualized confessions.

In fact, most of the talk-show segments Bennett rails against are as much moral fables as his stories of hard-working bees and frogs, just less politely packaged. The messages from Jerry Springer, Sally Jessy Raphael and Ricki Lake are surprisingly pious: don't beat up your girlfriend, don't cheat on your mate, don't betray your best friend. Those who confess to doing the above suffer TV's equivalent of the Inquisition: they are regularly hooted, denounced and lectured by studio audiences. Bennett and a few of his political buddies are perhaps the only people in America to take these programs so seriously, anyway. Some shows touch the lives of individual viewers, but many are so exaggerated and surreal, so clearly approached as social entertainment and fantasy, that the suggestion of serious influence on the young or anybody else would be laughable outside the context of the culture wars.

In *Don't Tell the Grown-ups: Why Kids Love the Books They Do,* critic, novelist and Cornell professor Alison Lurie reminds us that the stories kids cherish most have always been subversive. Jo March of *Little Women* was practically a radical feminist, given the post–Civil War values of the day. And it's easy to forget that the classic "Little Red Riding Hood" concludes with both the heroine and her grandma eaten alive, a denouement Bennett might find a bit reflective of the "underside."

Lurie writes that when she asked a class of her students which character in *Peter Rabbit* they would elect to be, they disdained Flopsy, Mopsy et al. and "voted unanimously for Peter, recognizing the concealed moral of the story: that disobedience and exploration are more fun than good behavior, and not really all that dangerous, whatever Mother may say."

Most of the great works of juvenile literature are rebellious or dangerous in one way or another, Lurie explains. "They express ideas and emotions not generally approved of or even recognized at the time; they make fun of honored figures and piously held beliefs; and they view social pretenses with clear-eyed directness."

Definitions of subversion and danger change, but this familiar drama—ringing adults' bells via in-your-face youth culture—always has the same twist: each generation of adults tends to forget its own earlier need to do the same thing. Grown-ups take the bait every time.

In all the thunderings about rap, journalists rarely point out that most purchasers of rap CDs are not angry inner-city kids—they're white suburbanites wanting to sound like angry inner-city kids. Perhaps the most appealing quality of the music they buy is the way it sends their parents up the wall. Morality tales that make parents and teachers beam is the very last thing they want—or maybe even need.

This cycle of boundary-stretching, followed by parental and societal—even governmental—overreaction, is what creates such a vast market for the William Bennetts of the world. Such conflicts fuel the largely mythical idea that because we have all this strange culture, we have all these problems—like violence. Yet the opposite seems true: Our society has lots of problems, which kids' culture reflects. Add the normal need of children to differentiate themselves from their elders and the volume goes even higher.

Kids have the machinery and the will to define their own culture. As fat as Bennett's books are, as stubbornly as they cling to the best-seller lists, they don't stand a chance of stopping or denting it. In fact, although Bennett crowed about his vanquishing of Time Warner, his anti-rap campaign seems as effective as his war on drugs or his efforts to improve education. Tha Dogg Pound's *Dogg Food*, the album that led to Time Warner's divesting itself of Interscope records, topped the music charts. The Death Row/Interscope CD sold nearly twice as many copies as its nearest competitor.

Moral: You still make them dizzy, Miss Lizzie.

A LEGACY

Bennett is not only a bully but an especially cold-hearted one when it comes to children, for whom his concern is as selective as it is lucrative.

Whatever its pros or cons, the conservative Republican agenda Bennett has advanced and fights for is not associated with providing any real succor or comfort to the many American children in need.

Marian Wright Edelman, head of the Children's Defense Fund, says the nation is passively witnessing an unprecedented assault on the few children's services available. "There is a national guarantee of some decency," she told a *New York Times* columnist. "No seven-year-old will have to sit in class without eating all day, his attention wholly distracted from learning by his hungry belly. No five-year-old will have to grow up on the streets or in an orphanage simply because her father left and our patience with her mother's inability to find and keep a job has run out." Republican budget cuts advanced by ideologues like Bennett, she warns, will eliminate even those minimal promises.

But preserving basic services for children is not a fight Bennett chooses to become a part of. Perhaps those hungry children can read, from Bennett's book, "All God's Creatures Have Work to Do," a story of two cousins, one industrious, one lazy. (You'll never guess how it comes out.) Bennett's moral: "This clever tale from southeast Asia helps us learn the difference between first-rate work and second-rate effort. It is good reading before starting a job." Getting the job is, apparently, not his concern.

Nor is it clear how the youthful victims of gun violence, more dangerous by far than CDs, might benefit from access to Bennett's thirty-dollar treasuries. Nowhere in his massive trilogy, of course, does Bennett mention guns. Republicans have consistently opposed even minimal gun-control legislation.

The image of a society lining up to buy books of moral fables to teach kids how to be moral and simultaneously writing off its neglected children ought to be vivid, even for someone like Bennett. He had the power to actually improve children's lives.

Instead, his primary impact on the lives of kids is to get them dragged into classrooms, auditoriums and living rooms to endure endless truisms and parables. ("Lord, Bobby, your homework is nothing. When I was a kid, they made me sit in assembly for hours and listen to stories from this guy named Bennett about bees and froggies . . .") He will be long and bitterly remembered for this.

Chapter 4

THE BIG IDEAS

Media have always moved in spasmodic cycles, with great leaps forward followed by periods of stagnation, then further leaps. The most recent cycle was, and still is, a whopper. A decade ago, most of us were reading a friendly daily paper and a newsweekly and occasionally tuning in to CNN; now we find ourselves in the midst of a volcanic information eruption. If history and common sense are any guide, however, we are drifting toward the end of this phase of the Information Age. Although all sorts of creative spurts will continue, we can already sense the beginning of a pause. The Darwinian logic of media makes some sort of breathing room inevitable. What we really need is an Age of Digestion.

Think about it: a few years of information stasis. The God of Media waves a wand and everything freezes and we finally get the time to look it over. It's an appealing idea. We would read all those manuals that came with our computers, maybe even learn to program our VCRs. We would take the time to look at some of the great new work on CD-ROM. We would figure out just what's on all those cable channels—the History Channel, the Food Network, E! Computer companies could slow down long enough to employ a few people to explain and service their products in real time on the telephone, just like other companies do.

We could get beyond America Online to explore some of the tens of thousands of computer bulletin boards we've never had time to dial up. We could venture slowly out onto the Internet and gawk at the brilliant, idiosyncratic sites popping up all over what's called the World Wide Web—combinations of text, graphics and electronic links that invent new forms of biography; cultural and countercultural electronic magazines and galleries; large and small businesses; attempts at community.

We have a lot of catching up to do.

Journalism has not been helpful. It's blown the biggest story in its own universe. Journalistic accounts of the new world have succeeded only in making us culturally schizophrenic: people can't figure out whether to smash their computers or to hide them from the kids or to rush out and buy new ones.

After years of either ignoring or attacking new culture, the old news media have turned zealous in the historic manner of the newly converted. Old media are so anxious not to be left behind and so excited that they have lost all proportion, drowning us in waves of confusing hype and breathless announcements about

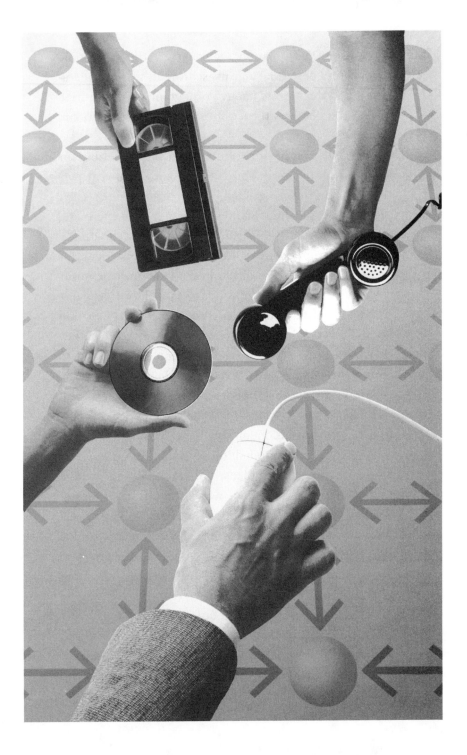

nonexistent information highways. At the same time they sound continual alarms, scaring us with exaggerations and distortions about pornographers, brain-fried kids and teenagers turned into Ted Bundys by rap and animated cartoons.

Journalism has a dreadful record of predicting our cultural and information futures, and little real perspective on covering itself. As an institution it can't even figure out how many homeless people there are, let alone predict the future. Newspapers thought TV was an insignificant, trivial form of amusement for years. Cable was literally a joke. New musical forms like rock, hip-hop and rap and music videos were dismissed as distasteful or dangerous fads, rarely spotted as the powerful political and cultural forces that they became. Old news media almost universally failed to foresee the dimensions of the post–World War II information revolution: the decline of newspapers and mass-circulation magazines, the emergence of new media, the evolution of the digital culture and the changing information habits of the young.

So we have two choices: We can cluck and whine about their inadequacy, or we can figure the information revolution out for ourselves, trusting our own experiences and common sense. It turns out that in this arena our instincts are probably as good as theirs.

Middle-class consumers, take heart: You are more powerful than you know. The nerds only *seem* to be calling the shots, cranking out smaller laptops every month, outdating software before you've really figured out how to use it, peddling complicated Internet-access programs and ever-faster modems. It's really up to you. Those of you with credit cards and bank accounts and kids will ultimately decide, as always, which new media stay and which go.

As usual kids are driving much of this change, creating, reshaping, and mastering the tools of the information revolution. And, as usual, they are getting little useful guidance from bad reporting about exaggerated dangers, or from phobic parents clucking about lurking predators instead of offering rational support. But, powerful as they are, even kids don't ultimately determine the fate of media in middle-class America. Their parents do.

New forms of media are legitimized when businesses incorporate them (the Internet), when middle-class families decide they need them (cable news, home-shopping channels), or when the children of the middle class can use them for education and fun (encyclopedic CD-ROMS, computer games). When media appear in tens of millions of family rooms and bedrooms, or on office desks, they matter. Until that point, they're just exciting cultural fads that may or may not make it to the end of next year.

For example, some of the most exciting and creative work in any medium is occurring on the World Wide Web, a series of graphically and textually linked Internet sites. There, corporations, politicians, artists and writers, and ordinary folks have launched a great flowering of personal expression. But it is still far from clear whether the Web will exist as a sort of digital magazine environment filled with graphically arresting little niches for small audiences or become a mass-market, mainstream medium.

On the other hand, computer-conferencing systems like America Online, the WELL or CompuServe, all of which seemed exotic and remote at the end of the last decade, have become mainstream media in every sense of the word. They make money; they present all kinds of information and breaking news from existing print media; their membership is affluent and well educated. Grandmothers trade health information online; gardeners talk about planting bulbs; shrinks compare their patients' symptoms; tens of thousands of citizens argue about politics.

The Internet is no longer anything like a "fringe" medium, although, as is often the case with techno-hype, nobody knows for sure how many people are wired. According to Nielsen Research, which had to scale down its estimates after researchers challenged its sampling methods, more than twenty-four million people over sixteen in the United States and Canada have access to the Internet and actually used the Net at some point in the three months prior to the survey, most of them through work. Other researchers have put the number of Internet users closer to ten million.

Even Bill Gates, in his best-selling book, *The Road Ahead,* cautions against Net inflation, noting the high attrition rate among online subscribers, for example. Whichever figures are correct, most surveys show the number of Net users zooming.

Over the next few years, we'll all get to see what survives and what doesn't. Whether papers will finally accept reality and radically change or whether they prefer to die. Whether commercial broadcasting continues as a force for original programming. Whether cable finds things to put on all those channels. Whether digital technology becomes cheaper, easier to use, essential.

Though we're are all made to feel as if we're falling behind, the dirty little secret of modern media is that nobody can keep up with everything. As a culture, we can handle only so much. And we are at our outer limits.

It's sort of stunning when it finally becomes clear that nobody really has a clue. Every corporation, every politician, wants a piece of the pie, but the menu changes three times a day. If the mythical information highway ever does get built, corporate corpses—along with the emptied bankbooks of smarty-pants investors—will line the road every step of the way. The first casualties—newspapers, TV networks, old-style magazines—are already piling up, but that's nothing compared with what will come. The great shakeout is at hand.

NOBODY KNOWS NOTHIN'

Americans understand that the way information travels is radically changing, and that this has deep implications for education, culture, politics, work and our children's lives. Still, you don't need to know much about the details. You watch CNN without understanding satellite technology. It's one of the great miracles of capitalist America: You can use all sorts of complex things, from cell phones to CD players, without thinking about what's inside them. So why do you need to know what makes the Internet or a cable modem tick? You don't. You need to know what good it is to you.

For all its aura of high-tech glitz, computer technology remains stunningly primitive in lots of ways. Imagine buying a car and dragging it home yourself in boxes. Imagine having to assemble it, using arcane manuals, staring glumly at wires, tires, valves and parts. If something goes wrong—and something always goes wrong—you call an 800 number and listen to recorded music for hours until some person you'll never meet comes on the line and guesses at the problems.

Every three months you see in the paper or on TV that the car you bought is outmoded, that you need pricey parts to bring it up to speed. After six months, it's clear that the newer machines can do all sorts of things yours will never be able to do, even with expensive upgrades.

Very soon, however, the machinery of the new media will be packaged and sold in simple, reliable, accessible formats. You'll buy something that looks very much like a television but it will have everything you need tucked neatly inside, accessible through some sort of super zapper/keyboard control. You'll take it out of the box and plug it into an electric socket and a phone jack (though wireless technology will eventually make even that unnecessary). The control will call up commercial and cable channels, home-entertainment systems, e-mail, reference material, banking, online services, movies, shopping channels, and Web site directories—all things already in widespread use—probably using icons that you'll simply push or click on. Simple, graphically enhanced menus will walk you through the functions step-by-step, much as advanced VCRs now do. Smaller, "baby" PCTVs can go in bedrooms and studies.

The past few years have belonged, perhaps for the first time in history, to the nerds, programmers, hackers and heroic free spirits of the digital world. But the nerds can't expect to stay on top too long, given the way the world works. America's genius for market-driven packaging and assembly-line production—the tradition that made phones, cars and TVs staples of almost every American household—will kick in. The machines will get cheaper each year. The profits, as always, will be in the options. You'll spend time haggling with the salespeople: Basic commercial service? Twenty-two inch monitor? Web browser? Home alarm system? Answering machine? Your own home page? Each will cost extra.

Upgrades, new products, additional software, will be transmitted and installed through fiber-optic lines coming into your house, or perhaps through cable modems, through disks inserted into slots, or some other no-heavy-lifting method of transmission. Repair and programming people will come to your house when you have a problem.

You'll probably have a second worksite elsewhere in the house or apartment and perhaps a smaller version for your kids, with controls like timers and blocking software to screen out violent or sexually graphic material, if you find that worrisome. There will be different models of this basic box for different uses: work, play, young users or elderly ones.

Otherwise, life will function in remarkably the same way it does now. The occasional pornographer will strike online, just as he does now on newsstands or in video stores. The occasional disturbed copycat will see or hear something that makes him or her do something dreadful. Some troubled kid will occasionally rifle through your e-mail, leave annoying messages on your answering machine, or figure out how to break into some government or corporate computer. When that happens, you can count on what remains of the old media to exaggerate the threat.

But the Republic will stand. You'll still have dinner with your friends, see some movies in theaters, read magazines, commute to work, buy books, sniff the flowers. The earth will still revolve around the sun.

When the time comes for you to buy this new equipment, you'll need to figure out exactly what's on it and what you want to use it for, just as you now decide if you want to spring for a sunroof or leather seats. Until then, chill. You don't need to know about PPP configurations. The technology involved has already advanced substantially since these words were written. Gassing about machinery obscures the things you do need to know, the one or two ideas that are driving many of these changes, the elemental notions lost in the hoopla. To wit . . .

INTERACTIVITY

Perhaps the single biggest idea is this notion of "interactivity," one of the words we hear so frequently that they've become background noise, but that we don't really understand. Interactivity isn't about machinery; it's about our relationship with information.

Interactivity—sometimes called "conviviality" by new media theorists—is the participation of individual users in their media. A revolutionary concept for modern America, interactivity will prove the enduring legacy of new media, the powerful force driving and shaping the cultural conflicts we're engulfed in. Interactivity is already reshaping politics, altering the consciousness of the young, sparking a return to media and politics by millions of people long shut out. Interactivity is the big idea our existing news organizations have been slowest to grasp, the pill so bitter many would rather perish than swallow it.

If you're over thirty-five, you probably grew up with noninteractive, or "passive," media. The daily paper came to your door in the morning (evening papers have been dying off for decades). You read what you wanted and ignored the rest. You had no say in determining the content of the paper, and unless you were intensely political or especially outraged, you probably never thought of trying to communicate with it. Nor did its editors think much about hearing from you. Each party's role was clear: They got to pick the stories. You got to read them.

If you read *Time, Newsweek* or *U.S. News & World Report,* the process was similar, except it happened once a week. The magazines were put together by nameless editors in Washington and New York, and "interacting" with them was even tougher than with local newspapers. If yours was among the more than 90 percent of American households that once watched an evening newscast (the number has now fallen below 50 percent), you had no chance at all of being heard or listened to. You were offered a choice of three newscasts, all strikingly similar.

The information world of the 1990s bears little relationship to that one, which feels as remote as ancient Babylon. Remember those Nintendos and Segas that attached to TV sets and riveted your kids? They were some of the first interactive (and digital) tools we saw. Although typically denounced as hypnotic, violent and mind-numbing, many of the games were sophisticated and challenging. They required kids to actively participate rather than passively watch. Often played in groups rather than individually, they involved social skills and strategizing. They required hand-eye coordination. They could be intensely stimulating, sometimes even addictive. And kids loved them; they took game playing to new levels of engagement and imagination.

And channel switchers—"zappers"—might be the most subversive political gadgets ever invented. Along with VCRs, they were a network mogul's worst nightmare. For decades, broadcasting was owned and operated by three men—William Paley of CBS, David Sarnoff of NBC, and Leonard Goldenson of ABC. We saw only what they wanted us to see, when they wanted to show it to us. Zappers and VCRs broke their grip, giving far more control of the world's most powerful new medium to the people who use it.

TV viewers didn't have to watch ads anymore if they didn't want to. They didn't have to watch boring programs anymore, either; they could instantly shop around. They could go bowling and watch *Melrose Place* on tape later, fast-forwarding through tiresome commercials and station breaks.

Add the development of satellite technology, which made CNN possible, and the unleashing of many-channel cable, which brought real diversity to programming, and the transformation of television was under way.

TV is our most underappreciated medium, mostly portrayed in terms of stupefying children and inciting violence, the proverbial vast wasteland.

But it is a phenomenal thing. A TV set is easy to install and lasts for years. It brings the whole world into your house, using little power. Lightning storms and freak accidents aside, it turns on every time you want it to, producing clear color pictures and good-quality sound. It costs a fourth the price of a good computer. It can occupy and amuse kids, show the Oklahoma City federal building minutes after a bomb explodes, and go around the world to wars, cultural events and volcanic eruptions. It shows great old movies, history, drama and—yes—lots of trash, too. Far more popular, enduring and important than most people acknowledge or realize, it is becoming one of our most interactive forms of communication.

As we've watched in wonder, the TV has mutated into a full-blown information, amusement and communications center. The "couch potato" is an outdated myth. TV viewers are now entertainment producers and directors. They have options, controls, choices and machinery to run—even products to buy, surveys to vote in, questions to pose, numbers to call.

Cable news—especially CNN—is a prime example of how interactivity is determined by content as well as machinery. In the 1980s, with most women in the workforce and nobody waiting at home to cook dinner for Dad, fewer and fewer families could plump down in the living room to watch the evening news for half an hour. But CNN was on twenty-four hours a day, offering continuous news, not news when David Brinkley or Dan Rather was available to provide it. CNN met viewers' needs, not the networks'. The fixed-time newscast—a longtime staple of commercial broadcasting—began to decline, in the morning as well as the evening. Since 1980, the evening news programs have lost almost half of their viewers.

Notice, too, how many cable broadcasts have built interactivity into their programs. No network newscast or major newspaper would dream of having a viewer or reader pose a question to a politician. What could an ordinary Joe possibly know, compared with a professional journalist? But from C-Span to MTV News, from E! to *Larry King Live,* interactivity—formats and technology that permits viewers to express themselves and participate—was part of the design. Many of these networks and broadcasts featured call-ins, phone polls, fax numbers and voice-mail lines, as well as special phone lines for additional information.

On cable, traditional boundaries between news and entertainment began to blur. MTV News helped register more than a million young voters in the 1992 presidential campaign with its "Rock the Vote" campaign. Comedy Central offered gavel-to-gavel spoofing of the presidential nominating conventions; its commentators were more blunt than any Big Three correspondent about Pat Buchanan's inflammatory speech and how it would hurt Republicans.

And in digital new media, interactivity isn't an added feature, it is the point. Online users have far more control over what they consume than any newspaper or mainstream magazine reader ever had. Online, people are constantly perusing menus, making selections. They can get news or go to live "chat" rooms, exchange e-mail or meet in groups to hear and question guest speakers. They can create new topics of discussion or respond to others'. They can pray with other members of their faith or—on certain "adult" boards, with the help of a credit card—download pornography.

Their loss of control has been jarring to our traditional media and political organizations, who had sat astride a tight monopoly over politics and news. They fought back and have been fighting ever since, complaining that these new, interactive media are dangerous and destructive of public discourse. New media have brought with them enormous cultural displacement—the journalists, producers, publishers, editors and academics who controlled most of our information flow have all been, to varying degrees, pushed aside. They don't like it.

Yet if some of the technology promoting interactivity is spanking new, the idea behind it has a long history. Our original press, founded by Tom Paine and his fellow hell-raisers, was highly interactive. Citizens ticked off about issues hung their arguments up on the sides of buildings. The press then was filled with individual voices.

If the founders would be horrified by Olympian journalists and corporate-owned media conglomerates, however, they'd feel quite comfortable with the raucous new media that permit lots of voices to pipe up, to speak directly to politicians and to one another. Our forebears would find radio talk shows familiar as well. An intensely interactive medium—such shows literally depend for their existence on people who call in—talk radio has grown from a couple of hundred programs in 1980 to nearly a thousand now.

The long, sad process of corporatizing the press, making users of communications media passive again, disconnecting journalists from the rest of us, has been under way since the eighteenth century. But in modern times, the estrangement has worsened. Reporters became wealthier and better educated, and reporting much more fashionable. For most of their history considered far too scruffy to hang out with "decent" people, journalists suddenly were living in Georgetown and summering in the Hamptons.

Watergate and Vietnam, both high-water marks of modern journalism, had the unfortunate side effect of intensifying the detachment. Having helped stop a war and bring down a president, journalists' collective sense of self-righteous purpose ballooned. Now reporters began seeing themselves as an unofficial FBI/morals squad, combing through the private financial and personal dealings of everyone in public life. That no one else in America—politicians, the public, historians— saw this as a suitable role for journalism didn't seem to slow anybody down. By the eighties, much of the press saw nothing but virtue in the *Miami Herald* reporters who staked out Gary Hart's Washington town house.

How could any institution so utterly disconnected from its consumers help but become arrogant and remote? And vulnerable.

Americans began ranking journalists lower than bankers and lawyers in public-confidence ratings in the late eighties and early nineties. The press's transparent pretense of objectivity didn't fool anybody, either. Sixty-seven percent of people answering a recent *Los Angeles Times* poll agreed with this statement: "The news media give more coverage to stories that support their own point of view than to those that don't." Polls by news organizations themselves, and by organizations like Harris, Gallup and Yankelovich, all show declining respect for journalism and rising anger over its intrusions into government and public life.

No wonder the environment was so receptive to new kinds of media. When America Online's news department asked its "readers" what, if anything, they would change about its presentation of daily spot news, readers suggested moving hourly updates to the top of the news menus. It was done instantly. They also complained that they didn't always want the pictures that accompany the text of breaking news stories, since downloading takes much longer when graphics are included. They were—again instantly—given the option to eliminate the pictures and just call up the stories.

Interactive media give their users a voice. Of course, CNN as an organization is still far more powerful than the people watching it. America Online is more powerful than its individual subscribers. Both have their flaws. But individual users have more clout—much more—than they used to.

✹

One of the things that make interactivity so big an idea is that it is critically important to the young, who have little experience with passive media. From Nintendo to cable channels to zapper-controlled TVs and computers, the young are accustomed to varying degrees of choice in all their media. According to a 1993 survey by Peter Hart Research Associates, three-fifths of people under forty-five, if forced to choose between cable or broadcast TV, would opt for cable, a remarkable statistic, given the limited availability and meager programming of cable just twenty years ago. The Hart survey found that "young people prefer choices. A majority of those under age forty-five believe more channels is a step in the right direction. The majority of those age sixty and older disagree."

The survey highlights one of the great generational divides fueling the wars over culture and media. Middle-aged and older people tend to be more reflexively resistant to change, often finding new choices disorienting, even unhealthy. The young can't get enough. Not surprisingly, the differences in the way these groups acquire information are stark, and widening.

The percentage of people under thirty-five who said they "read a newspaper yesterday" has plunged from 67 percent in 1965 to under 30 percent today, newspaper industry surveys show. The number of adults eighteen to twenty-four reading *Time, Newsweek* or *U.S. News & World Report* has declined by 55 percent in the past fifteen years, according to media consultant David Lehmkuhl. One confidential survey commissioned by a network news division in 1993 found that the percentage of viewers between eighteen and thirty-four watching commercial network newscasts has dropped nearly 50 percent since 1980.

A Yankelovich study says it all. Only 20 percent of people twenty-one to twenty-four watch ABC's *World News Tonight,* it found, but more than 30 percent watch CNN. And 35 percent sit down to savor *The Simpsons.*

The media business is complex; lots of factors determine whether or not ventures succeed. But one of the emerging realities is this: Interactive media—cable, talk radio, audience-participation TV talk shows, digital communities, Web sites, computer-conferencing systems—are mostly ascending. Traditional, passive media are either stagnant or declining. Americans increasingly are coming to see media participation—the opportunity to express themselves—as a right, not a gift conferred by the editors of letters pages.

At least magazines seem to have noticed this trend and have transformed themselves radically in the past decade, reaching for revolutionary new graphic designs, stronger cultural coverage, better writing with more point of view. *Time* and *Newsweek,* among others, have experimented with new formats and looks and have dramatically improved the range and sophistication of their coverage of interactive culture. *Newsweek* has a weekly cyberpage; *Time* was a major presence on America Online (now it's on CompuServe) and, via Pathfinder, on the Web. Even the venerable *New Yorker* began, rather grudgingly, to print occasional letters from readers.

Newspapers are a sadder story. The structure and presentation of daily papers have changed remarkably little. They still present "breaking news" we all saw on television the day before; they war relentlessly against the new culture of the young; they seem graphically impaired. Aside from offering unwieldy and clunky electronic versions online, newspapers remain in the grip of cultural paralysis. Not a single major paper has even put e-mail addresses at the end of stories so that readers can communicate easily with reporters, a simple addition most papers have had the technological capacity to do for years.

The same goes for the networks' evening newscasts, which today, as in the late 1950s, feature middle-aged white men in suits reading introductions to other people's stories for eight or nine minutes each weeknight. With information and newscasts emerging on cable, and hard-pressed Americans working longer and longer hours, fixed-time network news broadcasts have a dismal future, at least in their current forms. To date, none seem anxious to experiment with new ones.

JUSTIN'S PAGE

As much as anything, interactivity means attitude, stance, point of view. Interactive media are, in general, less formal, less institutional. New media don't speak in the stuffy voices of traditional journalism. From *Larry King Live* to MTV News to online communities, interactive media are ironic, outspoken, individualistic. Because the nature of such media requires them to communicate intensely with their customers, they are more responsive, in tune with their audiences. Thus it's no big deal when Clinton tells an audience questioner on MTV the kind of underwear he prefers, a statement that would seem shocking and improper at a White House press conference.

On mainstream Net sites like the California-based WELL, *Time* magazine on CompuServe, Pathfinder, HotWired (*Wired* magazine's Web site), on the electronic magazines Salon or Word, discussions are intrinsically interactive. So are the many thousands of pages and sites created by teenagers, artists, writers, programmers, designers and other one-horse producers of new media.

As an example of rampant interactivity, take a look at Justin Hall's Web page, Links to the Underground, which can be found on the Cyborganic Web site (http://www.cyborganic.com/). Justin's page is the antithesis of everything big, pompous and mean-spirited that mass media have become, and it suggests what interactivity can bring: generosity, outspokenness, candor and accessibility.

Hall, a Swarthmore student from Chicago, describes himself as a "speaker, dreamer, teacher, evangelizer." The idea that a young man's personal story would be told so graphically and well, and that thousands of strangers would care to learn about it—Hall's site averages nearly nineteen thousand "hits" a day—is astounding, unprecedented in mass media.

"I was born Justin Allyn Hall," the story of his life begins, "in Chicago at 12:01 p.m. on December 16, 1974, and until I was seventeen, I lived in the same house in the city's Northside."

When he mentions his brother, you can click on the underlined word "Colin" and see Colin's picture, along with a brief history of the fraternal relationship. You can, similarly, call up images of friends, girlfriends, and important places and things in Hall's young life.

"When I was eight," Justin confides, "my father, an alcoholic, killed himself. Much of my writing deals with this." So it does. Click on the mention of his father, and you can go to a page that describes and recalls him, complete with photo. Justin remembers looking at Colin, "watching him cry, and smiling, when we'd heard that my father had died. I was touched to see my tormentor moved to tears."

Using the textual and graphic links of the Web, you can penetrate as deeply into Justin Hall's life as you want to go. You can learn about his mentors, his life at college, the story of his arrest and strip-search while taking notes on a protest. His site generously leads visitors to other biographers and sites and offers detailed instructions on where to find other interesting works and how to start a Web site of your own.

The Web, writes Hall, "is the first semi-permanent unlimited worldwide exhibition space. Think of it as a never-ending world's fair." Putting lives online, he writes, "does not mean leading our lives online. It is about utilizing unprecedented sharing. We interact in the real world, and we use cyberspace to collaborate and share and conjure new possibilities."

All over the Web, people like Justin are telling their stories to one another, in stinging refutation of the idea that the Internet is a dangerous place filled with predators, thieves and perverts.

Hall's work illustrates powerfully, though perhaps unintentionally, what's lacking in conventional media.

No newspaper or newscast would permit this undergraduate to tell his story. Unencumbered by journalistic conventions like objectivity, Hall is free to speak his own mind. He seeks feedback and reacts to it quickly. No other medium is so anxious to teach other people how to participate in it.

LARRY'S SHOW

Larry King Live is a very different example of how popular interactivity is, and how distasteful to journalists.

Rather than forcing communications to pass through a journalistic filter, King's nightly broadcast on CNN dispenses with the journalist-as-interrogator. It permits viewers and guests to speak directly, first by giving the guest ample opportunity to talk, then by allotting a significant percentage of each broadcast to callers' questions. King remains cheerfully neutral, even detached, clearly seeing himself as a good-natured facilitator of communications between his guests and the public. Viewers perceive King's show as a medium that is responsive to and respectful of its audience. They ask the question as often as the host does.

Daytime talk shows are also inherently interactive, a factor in their success often overlooked by pious critics—here's Bennett again—shrieking about their vulgar content. The guest gets to tell his or her story and receives sympathy or scorn from viewers. The studio audience participates actively in the broadcast. Instead of sitting quietly and listening to the unfaithful husband pour out his confession, audience members hop up to demand answers or scold the offender themselves, often shouting at him to do the right thing. The host is not some omnipotent presence—as a network anchor or newspaper editor is—but shares his or her authority. Sometimes he or she gets overruled by the audience. Meanwhile, viewers at home can call in questions, fax in comments, suggest topics for future shows or volunteer to appear to tell their own stories. Talk-show producers are candid about how many ideas and guests emerge from their mailbags and fax machines.

Since interactivity requires surrendering at least some power to the viewer (or reader or computer user), the press has had a rough time with it. The idea that someone in Omaha can call Larry King on live television and ask a presidential candidate a question, which only reporters used to be able to do, is tough for journalism to accept. Reporters see themselves as the ones who are informed and tough enough to ask the hard questions.

Yet King's laissez-faire style can be as revealing as any interrogation. Ross Perot loved going on King's broadcast precisely because he could shoot his mouth off without being challenged. His paranoia and monomania revealed themselves a bit more with each appearance, and the broadcasts ended up limiting, not expanding, his appeal. If it were our only political forum, *Larry King Live* would be too narrow, too uncritical. But its value, in conjunction with other political coverage, is underappreciated.

The notion of an unreachable, untouchable press corps seeking the truth in the face of the public's hostility and indifference may be appealing if you're among the elite who get to ask the questions. But the country is unhappy with it, disenchanted with journalistic arrogance, turning to new media whenever they pop up. If a cereal manufacturer embraced the idea that he wanted his product to taste like fermented prunes whether the public liked it or not, he'd be out of business quickly. And as he filed for bankruptcy, he wouldn't get to blather on about the Fourth Estate.

MANY TO MANY

Another big idea. The traditional media embody the few-to-many communications model: a few editors, producers or reporters choose and produce stories that many readers and viewers consume. At its peak in the 1980s, CBS News had twelve hundred employees and was watched by tens of millions of people. A newspaper might have two hundred reporters presenting stories to an entire metropolitan region.

Ordinary individuals couldn't dream of owning the kind of press used to create a daily paper or the transmission facilities needed to broadcast the evening news. So the sort of cranky, opinionated citizens who founded the American press have been absent from it in twentieth-century America.

Partially because they are new, mostly because they are accessible by relatively inexpensive technology, new media have created a different model of communications: many talking to many. Justin Hall and ten thousand other college students telling their stories. Martha and Harry in Omaha calling Larry King. An elderly woman grieving for her deceased spouse messaging members of an online support group all over the country. Gun lovers fighting with gun control advocates on AOL. The idea that we can question and talk directly to one another, without relying on journalists as intermediaries, helps fuel new media's growth and transforms the notion of culture.

It portends a great leveling. The institutions of information are still powerful; they still set agendas. But individuals with access to technology are more powerful than they were, less dependent on others to provide channels of communication.

Although this many-to-many kind of communicating is routinely portrayed as disconnecting and isolating, it seems to serve much the opposite function. On most bulletin board systems (BBSs), anybody can suggest a topic. Anybody can answer a question. Anybody can support an argument or disagree with it. There is no middleman, no journalistic or other barrier through which ideas must pass. Sometimes, the resulting environment is raucous, disjointed or pointlessly combative. Sometimes it's just nuts. But quite often it is transfixing.

The politics forums *Time* operates on CompuServe offer the most intense public discussion in the country, far surpassing any letters column or op-ed page. Elsewhere on CompuServe, a father whose son is dying of leukemia opens a topic for parents whose children suffer terminal illnesses, and creates an instant community for himself and his son.

A gay kid in Nebraska messaged another in California that before he found the gay teen conference on his bulletin board, he felt such a "freak" that he might have considered suicide. Now, he said, he knew there were lots of others like him.

The elderly, long isolated in their homes and ignored by much of popular culture, pour onto America Online's Senior Net, where they can discuss loss, health, housing, or their kids and be quickly understood, since others are in the same boat. Many online seniors speak of how alone they felt before, how difficult it was to move about and meet like-minded people their own age. On Senior Net, romances blossom along with the advice and conversation; online connections are often followed by picnics and other face-to-face visits. In 1995, one Senior Net member suffered a stroke while posting a message. Her friends, accustomed to her writing style, noticed something wrong and called the police in her town. Later, as she was recovering, one of her online friends came to visit her.

One online discussion—via CompuServe—linked two groups at odds, veterans and gays. At the height of the debate over whether gay soldiers should be permitted to serve in the military, these two groups talked in conferences and e-mailed one another for days, an opportunity given few Americans on opposing sides of seemingly intractable issues like gun control or abortion.

This new capacity has brought us into something of a Prague Spring, mediawise. People can speak up again, like the early pamphleteers. And like those pioneers, they learn to take their lumps.

Online culture works against pomposity and self-importance. Newsgroups and conferencing systems are populated with plenty of quarrelsome deflators, and with people who use vast archives to correct errors. Academics, experts and analysts are frequently on hand (as I can personally testify) to challenge erroneous or glib assumptions.

Do all these many-to-many new media constitute a great leap forward? Hardly. They pose serious problems and challenges—and some features of the old media are worth preserving.

There are good things about newspapers, in addition to the obvious usefulness of movie listings and classified ads. A newspaper is portable and recyclable. It doesn't have to be plugged in, recharged or expensively upgraded every six months. The print no longer rubs off on your hands. Newspapers run those lists of candidates they've endorsed, which you can cut out and take into the voting booth on Election Day; while not fail-safe, this usually prevents your accidentally voting for convicted felons, well-known fanatics, or the recently deceased. The best newspapers offer something ultimately much more important—the analysis and context of the stories we all heard about on TV the night before.

A newspaper's front page offers visual and textual packaging that not only presents a story but gives a sense of how important the story is. No other medium handles local and regional news—tax increases, educational issues, environmental controversies—nearly as well. No other medium offers so strong a sense of place.

TV news, especially in its more modern incarnations, also offers much that's still valuable. We can see things live that we never used to be able to see until days or weeks later—trials, wars, Nelson Mandela walking out of prison, the Berlin Wall tumbling, Detective Mark Fuhrman taking the Fifth. The imagery is quick and clear. Despite all the complaints about dumbing down, TV (especially cable) is bringing us more political discussion in more places—on CNN, C-Span, CNBC, and MTV—than ever before.

TV still covers breaking stories like the crash of TWA Flight 800 or the Oklahoma City bombing better than any other medium has ever covered anything. Americans now take for granted—though it's unprecedented in the history of information—that when a story like that erupts, we will see pictures of it unfolding in real time. It's connected the world and affected our perceptions in ways we have only begun to comprehend. American popular culture, satellited into Eastern Europe and Asia, helped erode Communism and Islamic fundamentalism. TV provoked a worldwide response to the starvation in Rwanda, brought much of the nation to a temporary halt to hear the O. J. Simpson verdict. TV can be an extraordinarily unifying medium. We often have different reactions and interpretations, but at least we're all watching the same thing.

Traditional journalism's strongest resource is one that new media may never be able to duplicate: tens of thousands of mostly professional, trained fact gatherers and information presenters.

True, the structure of journalism serves them poorly. True, objectivity robs them of their voices, while their editors and publishers keep failing to change with the times. The nation's reporters are still far and away the most dependable force in public life for relaying events in some sort of manageable context.

Interactive audiences on TV and the flowering of individual voices online and on the Web are creative and exciting, but still chaotic. It is often hard to know who to listen to or what a person's credentials are. Journalists are observers trained in ways most other people aren't, skeptical of political and corporate posturing, skilled in acquiring information.

The ideal media world would incorporate both cultures: traditional journalism radically rearranged to become more interactive, graphically competitive, better written, more sophisticated, less hostile to the young; and new media giving full voice to individuals. Perhaps the most tragic consequence of the cultural wars is that they create a false construct: that one culture is superior to the other, that only one can survive and dominate.

The fact is, the two cultures complement one another quite well. Traditional journalism and its outlets remain the best medium for the coherent presentation of politics and civic issues. New media have proved superior at allowing diverse expression, transmitting fast-breaking news and popular culture, incorporating individuals into their structure.

People with modems and computers need never again be totally dependent on a few information outlets for their information. Their opinions—millions each day—pop up all over the Net and ricochet around the country. There can be enormous potential in the idea of blacks speaking directly to whites via this medium, abortion opponents talking directly to its passionate defenders, adults talking to kids. Old news organizations were often as much of a barrier between us as they were a vehicle for helping us understand one another.

Online, the many overrun the few, drowning out the spokespeople and lobbyists, elbowing aside the politicians and mediators. Sometimes the multitudes make a great noise that means nothing. But countless times each day they penetrate one another's consciousness, connect people to other people, broaden their understanding.

No existing online service, on the other hand, can sort things out quickly and reliably when a congressional budget fight threatens to shut down the government. For history, significance and context, you want a newspaper with a squadron of experienced Washington reporters. Such newspapers come cheap, and they don't need batteries.

Chapter 5

LET'S TALH (CALMLY) ABOUT
TALHING DIRTY

In contemporary America, nothing anyone can say—no educator, no shrink, certainly no writer—can calm down most parents about pornography, or make them comfortable if their kids are exposed to significant amounts of it. Resistance to explicit sexual imagery is entangled in deep-seated and intense social, cultural, religious and political traditions. Even sophisticated libertarians balk at the idea that sexual material should be accessible to children. This profound fear, even more than concerns about violence, drives much of the tension around the cultural wars.

With so many people locked in a reflexive cycle of outrage and fear—Oh my god, there's dirty pictures on the Net. Keep those bare butts off *NYPD Blue*—it becomes difficult even to discuss pornography. Politicians can't help exploiting this reaction, and journalists, clergy, eager-to-please media companies and frightened parents can't seem to stop abetting them—even though the research and literature about how dangerous exposure to pornography is or isn't is spotty and inconclusive.

Americans aren't ready to ask the tough questions about this issue: Just how dangerous are dirty pictures? Are our children really damaged by them? How much or how little exposure is a threat? Why are we willing to tolerate so much violence in our culture but so little sexuality? How can we move past this fruitless and bitter struggle to bar sexuality from public consciousness, even as the collective appetite for it seems to grow? How can we teach our children to cope with the availability of so much sexual imagery, rather than simply forcing them to pass it around behind our backs?

One thing that is changing, however, is the dawning reality that new media are largely uncensorable and pornography therefore largely uncontrollable, whatever the facts about its menace or lack thereof.

In fact, the federal district court in Philadelphia eloquently grasped last June what twitchy boomers, cultural conservatives and pandering journalists have missed for years. Its decision called the Communications Decency Act a "profoundly repugnant" affront to free speech and noted that the Net, as one of the freest and most participatory media ever, deserved as much protection as printed material, if not more. "Just as the strength of the Internet is chaos, so the strength of our liberty depends upon the chaos and cacophony of the unfettered speech the First Amendment protects," the court found.

The federal ruling was a rebuke not only to the stupidity and unenforceability of the law but to journalism, which has helped to create the hysteria surrounding popular culture. The press has fiercely fought for its own freedom over the years but rarely exerted itself on behalf of anybody else's. As a consequence of its short-sightedness, an institution conceived as a haven for free and unfettered speech has been shouldered aside—especially by the young—in favor of a much freer and more vigorous medium. The locus of free speech has moved to the Internet. In fact, the CDA turned out to be an enormous gift to the ascending digital world. A noxious and arrogant law, it was the equivalent of the Stamp Act for the digital community: resisting it conferred a common sense of political identity and purpose.

Just as some of the world's most repressive governments—Iran, China, the former Soviet Union—were helpless to stop the waves of e-mail and faxes that poured across their boundaries, so all the cops on the planet could not police the Net or the World Wide Web, on which billions of images, messages and pictures are transmitted daily. If adults and lawmakers understood the digital culture better, they would know this.

Kids can disguise online files under fake names. They can bury pictures in files that even blocking software can't detect. They can videotape graphic cable channels and pay-per-view movies, or get their friends to do it. They are at least as ingenious as their censors and, in these times, apt to be much more technically adept. Pornography will continue to be available—at local magazine shops, via online newsgroups and e-mail messages and, yes, sometimes through sex criminals and exploiters.

Our current approach isn't getting us anywhere. It isn't preventing pornography, or keeping it from our kids, or helping us confront simple-minded notions about sex and good and evil.

THE GREEKS DID IT WITH DOGS

Pornography is eternal. Like a river coursing toward the sea, it always finds a way around the obstacles desperately thrown up in its path. It dates back as far as recorded history. Los Angeles' Getty Museum offers a standing exhibit of exquisite clay vases from Athens, fashioned in the third or fourth century B.C., at the very height of classical civilization. Painted on the ancient artifacts are graphic depictions of homosexual and heterosexual intercourse, in almost every conceivable position.

And it's as strong a presence as ever, the passage of more than two thousand years of human civilization notwithstanding. "If Marx were functioning today," historian John Ralston Saul writes in *Voltaire's Bastards,* "he would have been hard put to avoid saying that imaginary sex is the opiate of the people.

"All around us there are illustrations of both soft and hard pornography: suggestive advertising, serious films and novels with obligatory carnal scenes, how-to books for better sex or more love or longer love and sexual fulfillment, books on finding the right partner through an evaulation of physical types or by colour charts or celestial analysis. Popular mythology has it that in the new, careful age of AIDS all of this is passé. But any cursory survey of films, magazines and books suggests that, as the fear of real sex grows, so does the use of suggestive images."

Though society and media struggle to come to grips with race, gender, culture and other social issues, we are almost immobilized by the very idea of porn. We just repeat the basic mantra, echoing a chorus of congresspersons, some feminists and other assorted alarmists: Pornography is unrelentingly evil; it's dangerous no matter where it appears; it must be rooted out.

Although pornography has been around forever, the idea that it threatens children is relatively recent. Social historians spot such notions beginning to circulate after the excavation of Pompeii, with its sexually explicit and licentious art works. The word "pornographer" first appeared in English in 1850, Saul writes.

Still, it took considerable time for the nasty stuff to percolate down. In *The Secret Museum: Pornography in Modern Culture*, Walter Kendrick explains that until the advent of modern media, pornography was the province of affluent men, the only people who could afford it or were literate enough to read it. Kendrick's book does precisely what journalism can't or won't do. He puts pornography in historical context and ponders the political and cultural implications of the ferocious efforts—from Plato's to outraged Victorians' to Women Against Pornography's—to control it. Though the nature and meaning of pornography have changed, says Kendrick, the underlying issues remain the same: power and fear.

"The first question they asked," Kendrick writes of the Victorians struggling to make sense of the dirty pictures from Pompeii, "was *What on earth were the Romans thinking of?* The second followed immediately: *What will happen if vulnerable people see these things?* The answer to the first question is still being worked on by classicists; the answer to the second came as quickly as the question: depravity will settle on women, children and the poor (they are predisposed to it); lust will flower in them (they bear its seeds already); they will rise up in wantonness, wrecking the achievements of three millennia—including us, their appointed guardians. Measures were taken. Gates were set up and guards were set at them, under orders to admit only grown-up, well-to-do males into the Secret Museum. Gentlemen could be trusted not to tear the edifice down, because gentlemen owned and had built it."

In the intervening one hundred fifty years, certain accommodations have been reached. The frescos and urns that so horrified those worried Victorians can be tolerated in certain contexts. Behind glass in a museum, for instance. "We now admit that the sight of a yard-long penis painted on a wall, or of a marble satyr locked in eternal coition with a marble goat, is unlikely to drive even susceptible souls to acts of lewdness," Kendrick writes. "We do so, in part, because we see such objects as 'art,' insulated from impact by the awe with which they ought to be greeted." But such contexts are few. Most of the time, we're still afraid of dirty pictures.

Modern pornography, as Kendrick points out, is radically different, more detailed, often more violent and degrading. Yet the indignation of the censors is eerily similar to that of the outraged Victorians.

So are the supposed remedies.

In 1857, the English Parliament passed the Obscene Publications Act, also called Lord Campbell's Act, designed to suppress "vice," which Lord Campbell called "a poison more deadly than prussic acid, strychnine or arsenic—the sale of obscene publications and indecent books." In 1995, the Congress passed a telecommunications act which made it a federal crime to disseminate "indecent" material on the Internet.

One element that has changed recently, however, is the expanding reach of the opposition. Not so long ago, crusades against "pornography" were waged largely by horrified clergymen, Southern congresspersons and other conservatives, while constituents on what we used to call the Left could be depended on to fight for free speech, to recognize that there was no reliable consensus about what constitutes decency or "filth." But today liberals, boomers, even some feminists, are demanding the right to define morality in their own terms, and to restrict the flow of information accordingly.

"We will know that we are free," writes Andrea Dworkin, one of the leading provocateurs, in *Pornography: Men Possessing Women,* "when the pornography no longer exists. As long as it does exist, we must understand that we are the women in it; used by the same power, subject to the same valuation, as the vile whores who beg for more."

Boomer parents and members of Congress may be the last people in America to grasp the uncensorable nature of new media. Children cannot be encased in protective bubbles. Computers, modems, VCRs, faxes, cellular technology, 900 numbers, twenty-four-hour cable channels, hundreds of magazines, make it as impossible to "protect" children from certain features of the real world as it is for the judicial system to find jurors totally ignorant of O. J. Simpson.

This is not as alarming as it sounds, though. The old media have made pornography seem a more ominous, ever-present threat than it actually is. And our own fears have probably made us more afraid of an occasional encounter with dirty pictures than we need to be.

THE TIME TEMPEST

The Great Net Hysteria of 1995 had been brewing for some time, but reached its zenith when *Time* published its now legendary "Cyberporn" cover, something of a Gettysburg in the raging battle of values between old and new information structures.

Beneath a computer-generated illustration of a terrified toddler, the headline read: "A New Study Shows How Pervasive and Wild It Really Is. Can We Protect Our Kids—and Free Speech?" The study was conducted by a Carnegie Mellon University undergraduate named Martin Rimm and was published in the *Georgetown Law Journal*. If ever a media organization was waiting for a survey, *Time* seemed to have been waiting for this one. Rimm's study, called "Marketing Pornography on the Information Superhighway," was "significant," *Time* said, because it told us as much about ourselves as it did about the dark side of computer networks—namely, that we are a nation of pervs whose children are at peril.

Since journalists are supposed to be objective and can't offer their own opinions, media organizations have increasingly come to rely on surveys, polls and studies to do their talking for them. Journalists can, with a few phone calls, instantly find studies supporting or refuting almost every conceivable point of view, along with legions of spokespeople, academics, lobbyists, nonprofits and fronts eager to "interpret" them. At least partly as a result, our civic debate increasingly resembles a statistical food fight, with battalions of spokespeople tossing numbers at one another.

Rimm, no exception, claimed that in an eighteen-month study, his research team surveyed 917,410 "sexually explicit" pictures, descriptions, short stories and film clips. On those Usenet newsgroups where digitized images are stored (Usenet is a global network of discussion groups), 83.5 percent of the pictures were said to be pornographic.

The survey also found a market driven by a demand for erotic materials catering to specific sexual proclivities, *Time* said: pedophilia (photos of nude children), hebephilia (pictures of sex involving youths) and "what the researchers call paraphilia (a grab bag of 'deviant' material that includes images of bondage, sado-masochism, urination, defecation, and sex acts with a barnyard full of animals)."

At first, the *Time* cover seemed a godsend for politicians riding their save-the-children campaigns, fearful parents looking for an excuse to turn off the computer and the usual cast of preachers, right-wing wackos, anti-porn feminists and Charlton Hestonites ready to deplore yet another facet of demonic popular culture. For much of modern media history, the story would have been read into the *Congressional Record*. In this case, something very different happened.

The study was challenged and debunked on the Net, primarily on the WELL and also on HotWired. The Net engendered a new kind of group journalism that questioned Rimm's facts and deplored *Time's* credulity, pulled in expertise from a variety of sources, spread a message of skepticism, provided instant commentary and analysis. The flap suggested just how ferocious the coming battle between the young and their supposed moral guardians is going to be.

Cyber-reporters, computer marketers, academics, researchers, programmers, legal experts and freedom-of-speech advocates on the Net (notably Brock Meeks, Washington bureau chief for *Interactive Week* and editor/publisher of CyberWire Dispatch, Donna Hoffman of Vanderbilt University, and Mike Godwin of the Electronic Frontier Foundation [EFF]) all worked almost reflexively—without planning, visible coordination, journalistic training or hierarchical editing—to disembowel the study within days. Not confined to a letters page published weeks later, these critics could share their own reporting and analysis immediately. The story "is an utter disaster, and it will damage the debate about this issue," Goldwin concluded early on.

Pornographic images, critics found, constituted only 3 percent of all the messages on Usenet and less than .5 percent of all images on the Internet. Rimm had apparently reached his 83.5 percent figure by focusing on a subset of private bulletin boards specializing in pornography, usually accessible only to paying adult subscribers with credit cards.

Such misrepresentations are often tough to challenge. But new technology presents new options: Journalists from dozens of organizations were also reading the attack on *Time*'s story in the WELL's media conference, facilitating a kind of fusion where boundaries between "new" and "old" media melted in pursuit of the story behind the Rimm survey.

Stories reporting the challenges to the study soon appeared in papers like *The Washington Post* and *The New York Times*. *Time* responded by publishing a short article that acknowledged the criticism.

The magazine cares about its standing in the digital world, and while it never retracted or apologized for its story or its lurid graphics (including one image of a naked man humping his computer), it did at least let its readers know about the questions being raised and acknowledged that it should have taken them more seriously. At the same time, Carnegie Mellon University announced an investigation of the way the study was conducted. And Rimm was dropped as an expert witness from the Senate Judiciary Committee's hearing on children and online pornography.

Furthermore, Rimm acknowledged that he had used the material from his Carnegie Mellon study for a proposed illustrated paperback called "The Pornographer's

Handbook: How to Exploit Women, Dupe Men and Make Lots of Money." Despite the imprimatur of two red-faced academic institutions—Carnegie Mellon and the *Georgetown Law Journal*—Rimm didn't hold up well either as a credible cyber-researcher or a child welfare advocate.

Time was not the only major media organization to take Rimm's bait. But because *Time* has been a savvy, visible presence on AOL and CompuServe and Pathfinder on the Web, and because its writers and editors have made themselves available online, it bore the brunt of the enraged digital response.

Aside from this new kind of cyber muscle-flexing and communal reporting, the *Time* fracas was interesting in other ways. Although the cover story suggested a major new danger to children, the story was curiously lacking in an element crucial to any good piece of phobic journalism: victims. There were none.

Time quoted the executive director of the National Center for Missing and Exploited Children as saying there have been "ten or twelve" cases in the past year of children "being seduced or lured online into situations where they are victimized." This is horrible for the victims but a tiny number, if accurate—evidence not of the dangers of the Net but of its relative safety. Of the more than seven million American households estimated to have online accounts in 1995, 35 percent included a child under eighteen.

In fact, the center's director, Ernie Allen, was quoted in the *Phoenix* (Arizona) *Gazette* as saying there are few cases of actual face-to-face contact initiated via cyberspace. The numbers are low, he said, because most children know or are taught not to give their addresses to strangers or agree to meet them.

Well-informed and prepared children sitting at their computers are vastly safer than many who walk urban America's meanest streets. With so dense a concentration of children online, luring them into dangerous situations should be like "shooting fish in a barrel," says Fred Cotton of Search, a computer crime organization. But it isn't, he says, because kids can grasp which situations are dangerous and which aren't, a view contrary to the image of the vulnerable child helplessly waiting to be preyed upon.

Statistics routinely get distorted and exaggerated to manipulate the media into paying more attention to issues, even issues that deserve attention, like homelessness and campus rape. Child-snatching statistics like the one cited by the *Time* story (800,000 kids reported missing every year in the United States) have long been used to frighten parents and children about danger from strangers. But Jennifer Allen reported in *Life* magazine in July 1995 what law enforcement officials have long insisted—such figures have been wildly exaggerated.

Allen quoted federal and other experts on child-snatching as saying that while 360,000 children a year are reported abducted, the vast majority are taken by a parent in a custody dispute. And that 100,000 of those missing children are kicked out of the house by their parents—"thrown away"—which suggests that parents at home are a vastly greater danger to children than predators online. Federal officials estimate that between 200 and 300 children a year are kidnapped by strangers who hold them overnight or longer. Of these, about 100 are killed. The numbers, say officials, are not increasing. Like stories of online criminals who attempt to lure children into meetings, reports of these crimes "grab headlines because it's so rare," says Gregg McCrary, a criminologist with the Threat Assessment Group in California.

That didn't seem to matter to the nervous parents *Time* quoted at some length. A Skokie, Illinois, parent forbade her three boys to sign up for Internet access, worrying that "they could get bombarded with X-rated porn, and I wouldn't have any idea." Another Illinois mother fretted, "Once they get to be a certain age, boys don't always tell Mom what they do."

The Skokie mother was not asked if she thought the damage from depriving her children of access to the Net—falling behind peers, being cut off from sources of information, failing to learn about what will surely become an almost universal communications tool— might outweigh any harm of stumbling across dirty pictures. Nor did anyone ask the other Illinois mom if she understood that at a certain age, boys—and girls—*frequently* decline to tell mom everything they do. Nor would it necessarily be healthy if they did.

It is not particularly easy for young children to access porn online, unless they're using credit cards liberated from their parents (not smart: odds of being found out are high) or from other adults (even less smart: odds of being prosecuted are considerable). Otherwise, it takes fairly sophisticated computer skills to locate and download dirty pictures effectively. Most kids who obtain a set are probably receiving them from their friends and classmates, not from predators and molesters.

What if kids do manage to find some porn? It makes sense that exposure to pornography can exacerbate the problems of already disturbed or dysfunctional people. It also makes sense that the peddling of pornography gives some criminals a motive for luring children and teenagers into dangerous or disturbing situations.

But it is far from clear that seeing occasional images of sexual behavior is in itself harmful to otherwise healthy children. There is little evidence to support the level of intense fear so many adults have.

The Brown University Child and Adolescent Behavior Letter of September 1991 cited a study of 160 fifteen-year-old males who were already showing signs of troubled behavior—they were referred from either the criminal justice system or social service agencies. Interviews with the teenagers included questions about the subjects' sexual, criminal and drug-abuse histories. Even in this atypical group, the researchers found, "the results indicate that looking at pornography did not increase the number of sexual crimes which the males committed."

"I AM SATAN, AND I'M BACK"

In *The Origin of Satan,* Princeton University historian Elaine Pagels points out that one of the cornerstone traditions of Christianity is the "conviction that although the believer may feel besieged by evil forces, Christ has already won the decisive victory. . . . The faith that Christ has conquered Satan assures Christians that in their own struggles, the stakes are eternal, and victory is certain.

"This apocalyptic vision," she explains, is a central idea in Western thought. It "has taught even secular-minded people to interpret the history of Western culture as a moral history in which the forces of good contend against the forces of evil in the world."

This ancient conflict echoes through the language, imagery and passion surrounding children and media. One brand of culture is good, the other satanic; one medium safe, another dangerous. The Mediaphobe continuously evokes evil in his battle to beat back the forces surrounding him—perversion, corruption, ignorance, debasement. But unthinking, centuries-old notions of good and evil bear little relevance to the cultural choices of the young. Nor do the prejudices and phobias of their parents.

Change is inevitable and pervasive. Short of the most Draconian kinds of censorship and Luddism, there is no stopping new media and their young consumers. Perhaps it's time to start teaching children how to cope with sexually explicit imagery rather than persisting in the fiction that we can make it evaporate.

Pornography has always served to break down barriers, dissolve differences, dismantle hierarchies. The "gentlemanly enclosure"—as Kendrick called it—was in part undone by Pompeian artifacts, lurid novels, graphic paintings. Today the new "gentleman," though sometimes female, still fights to prevent the ignorant and the vulnerable from getting hold of this dangerous stuff. And the fight is still pointless.

"Whatever its guise," writes Kendrick, "the pornographic urge remains unchanged—immune to argument, invincibly self-righteous, engorged with indignant
passion. If the twisted history of 'pornography' shows
nothing else, it shows that forgetfulness of history is the
chief weapon in the armory of those who would forbid
us to see and know."

Chapter 6

. . . AND ABOUT VIOLENCE

A central tenet of the Mediaphobe is that guns don't kill people; unwholesome movies, tabloid telecasts, video games and rap music do. That new media are not only corrosive and decivilizing but literally dangerous.

Consider Beavis and Butt-head, MTV's pair of repulsive animated geeks. In 1993, an Ohio woman blamed a *Beavis & Butt-head* episode after her five-year-old son set fire to their trailer home, killing her two-year-old daughter. The following year a watchdog group called Morality in Media said *Beavis & Butt-head* might be responsible for the death of an eight-month-old girl, killed when a bowling ball was thrown from an overpass onto a New Jersey highway and struck her family's car. The group cited an episode of the show in which Beavis and Butt-head loaded a bowling ball with explosives and dropped it from a rooftop. "We're not saying there is a connection," said a spokeswoman for the group, saying there was a connection. "But certainly the coincidence is difficult to ignore."

As a result of these and other widespread attacks in the press, MTV canceled the early evening showing of *Beavis & Butt-head* so that young children wouldn't see it. And the program's scripts have been supervised and sanitized ever since to remove controversial segments that might be blamed for inducing violence. The *Beavis & Butt-head* syndrome has come to typify the ways in which opportunistic politicians and eager journalists convince millions that culture, not social trauma, causes violence.

The 1995 firebombing of a New York City subway station was a classic example. Several would-be thieves squirted flammable liquid into a Queens token booth, causing it to explode. The clerk inside later died from his burns. The attack followed by two weeks the release of the movie *Money Train,* including a scene in which a pyromaniac squirts flammable liquid into token booths (though the celluloid clerks escape injury). *The New York Times* said the movie joined a "long list of films and television shows blamed for prompting acts of violence." It included the Martin Scorsese film *Taxi Driver,* cited by prosecutors as the inspiration for the attempted assassination of President Reagan by John W. Hinckley, Jr., in 1981; Oliver Stone's *Natural Born Killers,* said by the Utah police to have prompted a teenager to kill his stepmother and half sister; and *The Program,* blamed for the deaths of two teenagers because this 1993 movie showed drunken football players lying down in traffic.

Critics, reporters and politicians jumped on the *Money Train* parallels, with Bob Dole one of the first out of the gate. "The American people have a right to voice their outrage," he told reporters. "For those in the entertainment industry who too often engage in a pornography of violence as a way to sell movie tickets, it is time for some serious soul-searching." Dole, an opponent of gun control, did not comment on the M-1 carbine, with a clip holding seventeen cartridges, that was found at the scene of the fire-bombing. Nor did he have much to say when a couple of weeks later, the district attorney and the police said the attack had not been inspired by the film at all.

This distraction is not just a matter of journalistic harrumphing. It is a significant distortion of a major American social problem, with enormous impact on the way our society does—or doesn't—react to violence. "Americans have a starkly negative view of popular culture," *The New York Times* found in a survey taken in August 1995, "and blame television more than any other single factor for teenage sex and violence."

Twenty-one percent said television was most responsible for teenage violence, compared with only 13 percent who blamed lack of supervision, 8 percent who blamed the breakdown of family, and 7 percent who blamed drugs. In all, a third put the primary blame on some aspect of popular culture.

WHO'S GETTING HURT BY WHAT

As it happened, weeks before the subway attack, the Justice Department released a crucial report on juvenile crime. Nearly one in four people arrested for weapons crimes in America were juveniles (23 percent), the report said, compared with 16 percent in 1974. Such juvenile arrests more than doubled, from fewer than 30,000 to more than 61,000 between 1985 and 1993, while adult arrests for the same crimes grew by only one-third. Weapons offenses include the illegal use, possession, trafficking, carrying, manufacturing, importing and exporting of guns, ammunition, silencers, explosives and some types of knives. The statistics closely mirrored the surge in violent youth crimes, reported the federal officials. Teenage violence, particularly with guns, has been rising steadily since 1985, even as the number of teenagers nationwide has been declining.

But the Justice Department report got little attention in the media, compared with the furor over *Money Train*. It was the *Beavis & Butt-head* syndrome repeated, another purported link—advanced by politicians and the eager news media—between culture and danger. Even a meticulous newspaper reader or television watcher would naturally conclude that movies have more to do with violence than guns, poverty or drugs—and that without such graphic portrayals, the kids with the M-1 wouldn't have torched a token booth.

The fact is that during the past couple of years, as mediaphobes have decried the supposedly pernicious effects of pop culture, violent crime has decreased, not grown, in most of America. Homicides showed the largest drop in thirty-five years—12 percent—during the first six months of 1995, continuing the decline seen in 1994. In both big cities and suburbs, there were double-digit decreases in the murder rate. New York City, which has logged five successive years of declining crime, has returned to levels of homicide not seen since 1971.

If it weren't so pervasive an idea, the suggestion that those who watch MTV and talk shows or buy rap CDs are primed to commit mayhem would seem idiotic. Clearly, crime rises and falls for other reasons.

Yet violence among the young—who are presumed by mediaphobes to be particularly vulnerable to forces like lyrics and action movies—has been, sadly, on the rise. The urban underclass in particular—mostly black and Latino—has been engulfed in a wave of escalating violence. A slight dip (of less than 3 percent) in the juvenile violent crime rate in 1995, the first in a decade, shouldn't obscure that fact.

According to the National Criminal Justice Reference Service, homicide is now the second leading cause of death among young Americans. But it's hardly uniformly distributed. From 1986 to 1989, for example, the homicide rate for white twenty-to-twenty-four-year-olds was 12 deaths per 100,000. Among blacks, it was 72 per 100,000. Though black males age twelve to twenty-four represent 1.3 percent of the population, the FBI's Uniform Crime Reports for 1992 show that they experienced 17.2 percent of single-victim homicides. That translates into a homicide rate of 114.9 killings per 100,000 black males of that age, more than ten times the rate for their white male counterparts.

Scholars like Andrew Hacker, Christopher Jencks, Elijah Anderson and Cornel West have meticulously documented the origins of this tragedy—racism, disintegrating family structures, the rise of births among single teenage mothers, lack of job training and economic opportunity, deteriorating schools, the proliferation of weapons, the drug epidemic. Among the white suburban middle class, by contrast, violence remains relatively rare. And it is the affluent middle class, of course, that is targeted by marketers of CDs (including rap), cable and computer technology. Underclass kids can't afford computers or piles of CDs.

We know what's killing young people, and it isn't lyrics, cartoons or computers.

According to the Justice Department, 57 percent of young homicide victims are killed with firearms. In fact, between 1979 and 1989, the *non*-firearm homicide rate decreased 29 percent. Once again, the phenomenon is selective: In 1989 the firearm homicide rate among black males age fifteen to nineteen in metropolitan counties was 6.5 times the rate in suburban and rural counties.

In the debate over violence and culture, the White Rabbit seems to have become the moderator. Much of what we hear is the opposite of what our common sense and individual experience tell us. Violence among the young has escalated among underclass minorities. Violence among the more affluent young, the kids who use computers, watch a lot of MTV and are the primary purchasers of CDs, is rare, was never pervasive and has, in fact, decreased. The suburban middle class, of all ethnicities and races, is one of the safer groups on the planet.

Journalists understand the meaning of the chilling statistics as well as, or better than, the rest of us: Danger to the young is greatest among young urban black males, for whom the leading cause of death has been, for years, a bullet. This did not merit a *Time* cover in

1995, while Internet pornography did. The truth about violence in America receives only a fraction of the coverage given to "violence-inducing" new media. The media tell us more about violent pop culture—Snoop Doggy Dogg, say—than about the people who sell guns and drugs to children.

The history of crime and violence in America is little understood, rarely placed in context. But in *Crime and Punishment in American History*, criminologist Lawrence Friedman exhaustively traces crime and violence all the way back to Colonial America. More than two hundred years ago, Friedman writes, the criminals were primarily "men at the bottom of the heap." Recent studies by urban scholars like Hacker and Jencks have found similar patterns—that violent crimes are overwhelmingly committed by underclass men, with drug use, inadequate law enforcement, the disintegration of family structures, an epidemic of single young women having children and the availability of firearms all major factors.

Friedman concludes that the level of violence has stayed roughly the same and that the country has always refused to come to terms with it, preferring to sermonize rather than actually try measures that might work, from the Draconian (cutting off the hands of thieves) to the innovative (controlling guns, reshaping the police, legalizing drugs).

It's true: Americans would rather denounce representations of violence than attack the real thing. Yet, although conservative gurus like Dole and Bennett rail about the destructive effects of new media and culture, even conservative think tanks like the Heritage Foundation don't uphold their conclusions.

"Over the past thirty years," the Heritage Foundation reported in a March 1995 study, "the rise in violent crime parallels the rise in families abandoned by fathers." Foundation researchers concluded after a state-by-state analysis that a 10 percent increase in the percentage of children living in single-parent homes leads typically to a 17 percent increase in juvenile crime.

"Even in high-crime, inner-city neighborhoods," the report noted, "well over 90 percent of children from safe, stable homes do not become delinquents. By contrast only 10 percent of children from unsafe, unstable homes in these neighborhoods avoid crime."

The Heritage Foundation report never mentions TV violence, rap lyrics or other forms of pop culture as factors in the rise of violence in urban neighborhoods. What scholarly evidence suggests, the study concluded, was that "at the heart of the explosion of crime in America is the loss of the capacity of fathers and mothers to be responsible in caring for the children they bring into the world."

In fact, this very theme was sounded again and again at the Million Man March on Washington in October of 1995. "There's plenty of racism to fight," one black father told CNN, "but what we're talking about down here on the mall is that we are responsible for keeping our families together and saving our children from danger."

A Justice Department study called *Juvenile Offenders and Victims: A Focus on Violence,* released last year, also refuted misplaced boomer phobias and ignorant representations by critics of popular culture, offering a chillingly detailed portrait of violence among the young.

It is not a comforting report. While murder rates declined by substantial amounts in most age groups between 1983 and 1992, murder arrest rates for juveniles and young adults soared. And the report confirms again the disparity between white and black arrest rates among juveniles arrested for murder. Between 1983 and 1992, the black rate increased by 166 percent, in comparison with the white rate increase of 94 percent. Black youths—specifically black males age fourteen to seventeen—are far more likely than other juveniles to also be homicide *victims.* Young black males have the highest homicide-victimization rate of any racial/sexual category: twice the murder rate of black females, five times that of white males, and nine times that of white females.

Furthermore, in murder cases where the assailant is known, most juveniles (76 percent) were killed by adults, not other children, and 40 percent were killed by family members, most by parents. The Justice Department study also made clear, as have many others, the correlation between rising juvenile violence and firearms.

What's missing from this very comprehensive document? Any suggestion of a link between the violence it describes and pop culture—which indicates that journalistic coverage of youth violence has been consistently confused, incomplete or misleading.

The coverage of the *Money Train* incident was typical: Numerous therapists and psychologists decried the screen violence that "led to" real violence. In an audience of about a million, said one psychologist, perhaps fifty people will act violently who otherwise would not have done so, and the more exciting and graphic the violence portrayed, the more likely it will be to have an effect. It seems logical that some already disturbed people can be influenced by depictions of violence, but that is hardly what most parents or pols are worrying about.

"Beneath the huffy sound bites," reported *Newsweek* in an unusually nuanced story at the time, "lie nearly 40 years of extremely murky scientific research on the subject." Thousands of studies are cited by researchers. Really, there are closer to two hundred; the rest are rehashes of data. The press in turn reports the research uncritically, repeating, for instance, figures about how many acts of violence kids see each year without noting that the figures are derived from nature shows, cartoon violence and slapstick, along with grislier fare. A closer look at the actual research literature reveals that what we don't know about the effects of the media is often as dramatic as what we do.

The real outrage is that the more the media focus on pop culture, the less they—and we—grasp the real causes of violence. This kind of bad reporting permits people to be killed or maimed, a far more offensive consequence than anything Beavis, Howard Stern or Tupac Shakur could say or do.

TIPTOEING AROUND THE TRUTH

Why, then is this astonishing lie, this persistent effort to link culture with violence, presented to Americans day after day?

The most-prized consumers of media live in middle-class suburbs. They may watch in horror the bodies shown nightly in their urban-based TV newscasts, but most of the kids they're watching don't live nearby.

Although the media are frequently accused of racism in the way they cover blacks and whites, the truth is that modern media have no ideology. Almost everything they do is rooted in marketing and economics. Newspapers and TV stations rarely focus on inner-city issues and problems simply because there's no money in it; most people who live in the inner city don't spend enough money to attract advertisers. Journalism doesn't see any viable economic future in Watts or the South Bronx—the very neighborhoods where explorations of the real causes of violence would take place. The 1995 death of *New York Newsday* ended print journalism's most ambitious modern experiment to remain viable in central urban areas.

Because journalism does care deeply, as most profit-making commercial enterprises do, about the suburban middle class, it provides what it sees as a valuable consumer service by warning about new media, in the same way it would sound the alert about onrushing hurricanes, defective playpens or the latest cholesterol findings.

To be fair, journalists also receive confusing messages and pressures from African-Americans, many of whom argue that too much coverage of violence among young blacks creates unhealthy stereotypes. Far more whites commit crimes than blacks, they contend, but black crime is disproportionately covered. Blacks are also frustrated because their fastest-growing socioeconomic group—the middle class—rarely shows up on the news.

Such issues are volatile, often linked with other dangerous topics like race, the underclass, and immigration. The culture of political correctness has damaged journalism in visible ways. Reporters approach charged issues like race and gender only gingerly.

Journalism doesn't distinguish between middle-class and underclass crises because reporters don't like being accused of stereotyping minorities or the poor, as they have often been in the past. It's easier and more prudent to generalize about social problems, to present them as universal dangers, rather than sort through them and isolate the real sources and causes. Thus affluent suburban children are lectured endlessly about social problems that are far less likely to affect them directly than to harm their counterparts in poverty-stricken minority neighborhoods—illegitimate-birth rates, for example, and AIDS.

A number of affluent private schools participate in national ban-TV-for-a-week campaigns, distributing literature that claims American children watch an "average of seven hours of TV a day." Underclass children, whose (frequently single) parents can't afford day care or other supervised activities, are at greater risk of ODing on TV; few private-school children could survive for long in their schools if they watched that much television. But since journalism makes no class distinction concerning the victims of social plagues like violence, neither do we. So boomer parents whose children are safe and well educated panic at persistent reports of pornography online or violence on television, while the children who truly suffer are ignored by government and society.

As a profoundly middle-class medium, mainstream journalism lacks any economic incentive to cover the underclass thoroughly; in fact, news media that pay too much attention risk losing or alienating prized upper-middle-class consumers.

Finally, journalism has become addicted to studies, surveys, polls, spokespeople and lobbyists. Reporters have become fat and lazy relying on other people to do their talking and reporting for them. Issues like violence, race and crime are relayed almost entirely in terms of what proponents of specific points of view say about them. Our civic consciousness is paralyzed by checkmating arguments. How could we possibly reach anything like consensus when our primary information media don't permit their own reporters to reach conclusions, only to quote from spokespeople whose livelihood literally depends on never changing their minds?

Covering the true causes of urban violence would mean taking on some of the most difficult and sensitive issues in American life—race, poverty, welfare systems, law enforcement. Many journalists, like academics, have come to fear such issues; probing them inevitably brings accusations of racism or some other form of bigotry. Blaming violence on media and culture is easier and safer, both for journalists and for opportunistic politicians.

Besides, the structure, power and function of mainstream journalism are deeply threatened by new media, which are siphoning off viewers, readers, and ad revenue. By portraying new media as dangerous and decivilizing, the press appears responsible and safe in contrast. If nothing else, it feels virtuous. Maybe it thinks it will eventually convince others of that, too. So far, its prospects are dim; more and more, the young are abandoning what we used to call "the press."

PARENTS, PROBLEMS AND THE PRESS

One of mainstream journalism's modern tragedies, in fact, is the way it attacks new forms of media and culture, alienating their users rather than serving them and retaining them by covering their world well. Thus *TV Guide*—little more than page after page of small print of the kind newspapers have provided for decades—becomes one of the largest-circulation magazines in the world, while newspapers that preferred to sneer at television and declined to cover it now hemorrhage circulation and income.

Although individual journalists are pouring online, especially on increasingly fashionable conferencing systems like the WELL, journalistic institutions remain hostile to new media. Few editors watch *Jenny Jones,* or much television at all; even fewer understand the digital culture and its many offshoots. When someone offers a study purporting to show that the online culture is riddled with pornography and is dangerous to children, they are as happy to believe it and spread the message as they were to report that comic books threatened decency (in the forties), that rock and roll was dangerous (in the fifties), that video games turned kids violent (in the eighties).

Well-to-do boomers are profoundly anxious parents, and mediaphobic reporting plays into their deepest fears. Attentive to each new spate of warnings, they use them as rationales for further encircling their children in protective cocoons. Thus, cable and computers are not liberating, empowering, or community-building new media but menaces to be warded off by V-chips, blocking software and anti-porn legislation.

The conversations about the degradation and dangers of modern culture have become universal. I've had variations of this discussion hundreds of times in recent years with friends, neighbors, other parents and journalists:

THE CONVERSATION

Don't you think that rap and sleazy talk shows and *Beavis & Butt-head* are disgusting? I don't want my kids anywhere near that garbage. No wonder there's so much violence!

But do you know who the kids are who buy rap CDs and listen to MTV?

Who?

They're white middle-class suburban kids—overwhelmingly.

But you're not denying that the stuff is disgusting.

Maybe it is. But that doesn't mean it's responsible for violence. The rise in violence in recent years has to do primarily with underclass kids. The common threads are they have no fathers, they go to lousy schools, they have easy access to guns and they've grown up amid a drug epidemic. But they aren't the viewers that racy talk shows or *Beavis & Butt-head* want to reach, and they can't afford all those CDs.

But have you listened to this stuff? It's sexist. It's awful.

Maybe. But it has little to do with violence. Since you're so concerned about violence, tell me if you know how many kids were killed by guns in America last year?

I have no idea.

Look, I'll agree that some of this stuff is vulgar and offensive. Will you agree that it's astonishing to know so much about scary rap and talk shows but almost nothing about how many kids get killed each year and why? Or how they get the guns?

The conversation usually ends there.

Popular culture, using its many new means of transmission, has exploded. Some of the art, information and drama it creates—*NYPD Blue, The Larry Sanders Show, Law and Order*; CDs from R.E.M. and the London Symphony; CD-ROMs from artists like Pedro Meyer; museum Web pages; religious and political conferences online—is classy, even fascinating. Some of it—the nastiest rap lyrics, the dumbest talk shows, certain karate-kicking video games—is mind-numbing and offensive to adult sensibilities.

But grown-ups all seem to lose the neurological chip that enables them to call up their own youth. The point of much of adolescent culture is to be offensive, to individuate kids from their parents, to help define their own ideas and values. Popular culture has been helping them to do that for a good half-century now.

Adult America—astonishingly, including the very boomers who helped midwife rock and roll—takes pop culture literally, which is the worst and most useless way to approach it. Beavis and Butt-head are not advocates of stupidity but ironic commentators on it. The rhetorical styles of many rap artists are absorbed by listeners not as literal advisories but as more complex expressions of attitude, values and group identity. Oliver Stone's *JFK* was never meant to depict historical

truth; it was a prescient reflection of the angry paranoia which subsequently became unmistakable in
American politics. And Spike Lee's relentless poking is
intended as provocation, a challenge to both whites'
and blacks' views on race.

The problem isn't that popular culture is eroding our
civic and moral fabric, but that we take it far more seriously than its creators or consumers do; we give it
more weight than it deserves. There is no more evidence that teenagers who cheer on the riotous discussions of sexual betrayal on *Ricki Lake* then go out and
sleep with their best friends' friends than there is that
kids who listen to Ice-T go out and murder cops.

Concerns about how much time children spend un-
attended in front of screens, or locked in their bedrooms with computers, are perfectly valid. Good
parents always curb their children's unhealthy excesses, from overindulging in Chee-tos to joining a
pack of neighborhood vandals. But the notion that exposure to pop culture is inherently dangerous is un-
supported by research, statistics or common sense.
We lose credibility with kids by giving it such weight.
Most MTV watchers are safe, law-abiding, middle-
class children; they know quite well that exposure to
vulgar videos won't send them out into the streets
packing guns or into their bedrooms wearing leather
bustiers.

Years of battles over comics, rock and other forms
of youth culture seem to have left us none the wiser.
We take the bait every time. Rather than engage our
children in intelligent dialogue, we simply come
across as the pompous out-to-lunch windbags many
of us have become.

For black artists and audiences, the cultural issues are more complex. Expressions of anti-establishment anger and provocative lyrics about sex and violence are jarringly offensive to many adults, white and black, but seem an almost inevitable reflection of the anger, disconnection and violence in many minority communities. When thousands of kids are injured or die violently every year, how could the music their peers create be uplifting and "moral" in the tradition of William Bennett and parents whose experiences are so strikingly different?

One of the reasons we have so much trouble understanding complicated issues like purported connections between culture and violence—and why people like William Bennett can exploit them so profitably—is that so many "experts" are thrown at us, often peddling contradictory conclusions.

But some experts have better credentials than others.

Harvard psychiatrist Robert Coles, no fan of TV violence, has been studying and writing about the moral, spiritual and developmental lives of children for much of his life. His works have been widely praised and circulated as ground-breaking, insightful looks at kids' complex inner lives. Parents worried about the impact culture has on their kids should ignore the headlines and read *The Moral Life of Children*. They would know more and feel better.

A young moviegoer, Coles writes, can repeatedly be exposed to the "excesses of a Hollywood genre"—sentimentality, violence, the misrepresentation of history, racial stereotypes, pure simple-mindedness—and emerged unscathed intellectually as well as morally. In fact, sometimes these images help the child to "sort matters out, stop and think about what is true and what is not by any means true—in the past, in the present." The child, says Coles, "doesn't forget what he's learned in school, learned at home, from hearing people talk in his family and his neighborhood."

Culture offers important moments for moral reflection, and it ought not to be used as an occasion for "overwrought psychiatric comment," Coles warns, or for making banal connections between films and "the collective American conscience."

But it is. All the time.

This discussion—of culture, morality and violence—is made more difficult because of not irrational fears on the part of minorities that their children will be demonized and stereotyped as lawless and dangerous, when only a small percentage are involved in crime or violence. Understandably, black leaders want to project more positive images of African-American life than the young black men so often seen in handcuffs on the local news.

But black political leaders who insist that violence is a universal American problem equally affecting blacks and whites, or who point to media and popular culture as its primary causes, are hardly advancing any racial goals or staving off prejudice. They simply make it easier for the majority of Americans to ignore poverty, bad schools and guns—since those problems are purportedly less to blame than *Money Train*. Unwittingly, this particular brand of mediaphobe conspires to keep Americans ignorant about what really causes violence and what can be done to prevent it.

Chapter 7

MEDIA THEN: THOMAS PAINE

If any father has been forsaken by his children, it is Thomas Paine. Statues of him should adorn journalism school lobbies; his values should be guiding and sustaining the contemporary communications media through their many travails. Instead, he's become a fuzzy, marginal historical figure, remembered for one or two sparkling patriotic quotes—"These are the times that try men's souls"—but little else.

Paine's life would have tried anybody's soul.

He was detested in his native England, which viewed him as a traitor, convicted him of seditious libel, minted coins that graphically envisioned his hanging. Officials in France, whose revolution he eloquently defended, threw him in prison and came within hours of decapitating him. In America, his memory has been tended by a few determined academics and a stubborn little historical society in New Rochelle, N.Y., where he spent many of his final, impoverished days.

At the end of his life, he was shunned by the country he helped create, reviled as an infidel, forced to beg money from friends, denied the right to vote, shot at in his home, refused burial in a Quaker cemetery. His grave was desecrated. A popular old nursery rhyme about Paine could as easily be sung today:

> Poor Tom Paine! there he lies:
> Nobody laughs and nobody cries.
> Where he has gone or how he fares
> Nobody knows and nobody cares

Certainly that's true of the media. The modern-day press has become thoroughly disconnected from the professional revolutionary who, nearly single-handedly, promoted the concept of the uncensored flow of ideas and pioneered a new kind of communications—journalism—in the service of the then-radical proposition that people should control their own lives. His heirs have abandoned the fearless, democratic medium he envisioned when he wrote *Common Sense* and helped spark the American Revolution.

In fact, the sad part is that it's necessary to pause here and explain who Paine was.

Between his birth in 1737 and his death in 1809, enormous political upheavals—the development of democratic government, the American and French revolutions, the attempted reform of the British political system—transformed the Western world. And Paine was in the middle of them all, sticking his neck as far out as he could.

Paine was obsessed with spreading the word that people ought to be able to communicate freely and decide their own fate. He was one of the first journalists in America to argue that women and slaves should have the same rights as freemen, that animals should be treated gently, that the elderly should have financial security and that even revolutionary governments should be merciful to those they overthrow.

About the only things at which he succeeded were writing brilliantly, making enemies and spotting injustice. Otherwise, his life was a shambles. Paine worked as a stay-maker and customs collector in England and ended two unhappy marriages there. He lost his job and went broke campaigning for better conditions for his fellow collectors, setting a bad-luck pattern for the rest of his life.

Inspired in part by his encounters in England with Benjamin Franklin, he moved to the colonies when he was thirty-seven, bringing with him little more than Franklin's prescient letter of recommendation: "The bearer of this letter, Mr. Thomas Paine, is well recommended to me as an ingenious worthy young man." Barely a year after his arrival, he published what was and still is one of the most powerful pieces of political journalism ever written—*Common Sense.*

Common Sense popularized the idea of modern political writing, of open, reasoned challenge to entrenched authority, of broad public debate among masses of people rather than within a privileged circle. As a strong demonstration of the power of impassioned argument, *Common Sense* legitimized an outspoken press. The pamphlet was a passionate but logical and beautifully composed argument for American independence. But, just as important, it was one of the first persuasive arguments ever on behalf of the notion that monarchies, feudal states and dictatorships—the systems of government that ruled all of Paine's world—should give way so that citizens could determine their own fate.

Paine's battle cry was a vision of a new, more moral nation: "O! ye that love mankind! Ye that dare oppose not only the tyranny but the tyrant, stand forth! Every spot of the old world is overrun with oppression. Freedom hath been hunted round the globe. Asia and Africa have long expelled her. Europe regards her like a stranger, and England hath given her warning to depart. O! receive the fugitive, and prepare in time an asylum for mankind."

Contemporary journalism rarely advances these notions or makes much room for those who do. Yet Paine does have a descendant, of sorts, a place where his values prosper and are on display millions of times a day: on the Internet, his ideas about free expression are relevant again. Nearly two centuries after his death, in a form Paine couldn't have imagined but would plunge into with joyous passion, the Internet is, in many ways, the embodiment of everything he believed.

✳

The ferociously spirited press of the late 1700s that Paine helped invent was dominated by individuals expressing their opinions. The idea that ordinary citizens with no special resources, expertise or political power—like Paine himself—could sound off, reach wide audiences, even touch off revolutions, was brand-new to the world. In his wake, writes Gordon S. Wood in *The Radicalism of the American Revolution,* "every conceivable form of printed matter—books, pamphlets, handbills, posters, broadsides, and especially newspapers—multiplied and were now written and read by many more ordinary people than ever before in history."

Paine's friend Thomas Jefferson was, it turns out, a proto-hacker: "That ideas should spread freely from one to another over the globe, for the moral and mutual instruction of man, and improvement of his condition, seems to have been peculiarly and benevolently designed by nature, when she made them, like fire, expansible over all space, without lessening their density at any point, and like the air in which we breathe, move and have our physical being, incapable of confinement or exclusive appropriation. Inventions then cannot, in nature, be a subject of property."

Paine and his revolutionary colleagues saw in their new media the means of transmitting ideas and opening minds. It was part of the political transformation he envisioned when he wrote, "We have it in our power to begin the world again."

But Paine's brand of mass media was doomed from the outset. Never skilled in business, he didn't foresee how fragile and easily overwhelmed such forms of expression would be when they collided with free-market economics.

Today's media have little in common with that brief early outpouring. The modern press believes as an institution that *it,* not cacaphonous individuals, should set the nation's course. It shares power and access grudgingly, via letters columns, clunky online publishing experiments, tepid op-ed pages, person-in-the-street features and opinion polls. Otherwise, it jealously guards its control of the country's political and social agenda.

Where would the early pamphleteers—or Thomas Jefferson—write today? To get any real attention on TV or in the papers, they'd have to march, blockade or burn something, or try to get through to a radio talk show or Larry King. But if they had computers and modems, they could instantly spread their messages. Paine and Jefferson seem, eerily often, to be talking about this new medium taking shape. Anyone online can recognize the idea of countless ordinary people participating in the creation of public opinion, their ideas "expansible over all space."

If Paine's vision was aborted by, ironically, the new technologies of the last century, newer technology has brought his vision full circle. If his values no longer have much relevance for journalism, they fit the Net like a glove.

From tens of thousands of newsgroups to the vast public opinion forums growing on the giant bulletin boards, the Internet gives the old rabblerouser's unhappy spirit a place to rest.

❋

It is almost impossible, today, to imagine the impact of *Common Sense.* It's also, sadly, impossible to imagine contemporary journalism doing anything like it. Historian Gregory Claes, in *Thomas Paine, Social and Political Thought,* quotes a Colonial observer who described *Common Sense* as bursting forth "like a mighty conqueror bearing down all opposition." It became America's first best-seller, with more than 120,000 copies sold in its first three months, and possibly as many as half a million its first year—this in a country whose population was three million. Newspapers reprinted it. Common people quoted it to one another. With its challenge to hereditary monarchies, its argument for separation from England, it had an electric effect.

A corresponding success in 1995 would earn the author millions in royalties, rights, speaking fees. Paine, however, didn't earn a penny from *Common Sense*. He paid the cost of publication—forty pounds—himself, then donated the copyright and all proceeds to the colonists' struggle for independence. Royalties would make his work more expensive, he feared, and thus less accessible. This idea cost him, in the most literal sense: Paine was impoverished for much of his life.

Most of us long ago learned to immunize ourselves against the patriotic slogans offered by teachers and politicians. But when you give even the most familiar of these sayings a closer look, especially in their context, they can sizzle: "These are the times that try men's souls. The summer soldier and the sunshine patriot will, in this crisis, shrink from the service of their country; but he that stands it *now*, deserves the love and thanks of men and women." Reading Paine's work is like that. He makes these dusty old ideas come to life as the startling new ideas they were. And he seems to have our time in mind as much as his.

Not merely a paper revolutionary, he fought in the Colonial army as both a soldier and a mobile media warrior, pausing to write stirring broadsides. Then he returned to England, where he could not, of course, resist attacking the monarchy. Nor could he pass up a chance to write encouragingly of the revolutionary forces gathering steam in France. His essay *The Rights of Man,* an argument for natural and universal human rights, became a worldwide sensation; after its publication he was forced to flee England minutes ahead of officers carrying warrants for his arrest.

In France, as he worked to support the revolution, Paine's unerring instincts for enraging authority did not desert him. He urged the French revolutionaries to show more mercy, even pleading for the life of Louis XVI, and grew increasingly vocal about the betrayal of the revolution's democratic and republican ideals.

No one in authority ever loved Paine for long. The country's vengeful leaders branded him a British spy and deposited him for months in Paris's dread Luxembourg prison, where he watched hundreds of fellow prisoners get dragged off to the guillotine. On the day he himself was to be killed, supporters in the prison tricked the turnkeys into hiding the mark on the door that identified prisoners to be executed. The death squad passed him by, and days later the revolutionary government was overthrown.

The American government finally interceded in his behalf, and he was eventually released. It was time to move on. Mostly owing to Thomas Jefferson's graciousness, America accepted him—reluctantly.

✳

It's painful to think of Paine scrutinizing today's media. He'd hardly recognize the American press.

The leaders of American print journalism convene almost continuous panels and conferences to wonder *what we're doing wrong,* to address declining market share, defecting young readers and competition from new technologies. Journalism sees itself as being in a severe marketing crisis—too much competition from TV and cable, too many computers, too many tabloids, too few young readers.

But the press's crises seem to be moral as much as— if not more than—they are economic.

Journalism, in Paine's view, was an instrument of social change, a vehicle for passionate writing, a provoker of intense civic debate. It no longer serves any of those functions in any significant measure. Good writing has been bleached from papers and telecasts. Opinion is largely limited to the moderate center. Paine understood intuitively that journalists belonged on the outside looking in, and spent much of his life in isolation as a result. But in contemporary media centers like New York, Washington and Los Angeles, journalists are often part of an affluent social elite who have little connection with the people they are supposed to inform.

Not surprisingly, a *Times Mirror* poll last year found that many Americans see the media as a "powerful destructive force, inflaming the national mood of anger and political alienation."

Paine would not accept payment to write about any subjects but those he personally cared about, even when he needed money badly. He could easily have had the cast of McLaughlin and Company or *Crossfire* in mind when he wrote, "The wretch who will write on any subject for bread, or in any service for pay . . . stands equally in rank with the prostitute who lets out her person." He argued that journalists should never become an elite. In an essay on press freedom, Paine warned against the idea, "common with printers, especially of newspapers," that those who own and operate a press are entitled to more privileges than others. Perhaps Paine's biggest journalistic idea was that the purpose of the press was to raise the toughest questions society faced.

He believed that public institutions all need moral underpinnings and he never stopped trying to articulate them.

✳

In fact, nothing could stop him.

When Jefferson invited him to come back to America after fifteen years in Europe, he returned to a society already very different from the one he'd left. The country had become profoundly less revolutionary, and evangelical religious elements much more powerful.

Federalists—at the time political opponents of Jefferson, along with the reactionary clergy and antidemocratic social and political organizations—were outraged at his return and launched a series of attacks that continued until and beyond his death. Philip S. Foner, in his introduction to a collection of Paine's writings published in 1945, recounts some of the epithets applied to Paine: he was called a "lilly-livered sinical rogue," a "demi-human archbeast," an "object of disgust, of abhorrence, of absolute loathing to every decent man except the President of the United States."

Many of Paine's former friends avoided him, citing his inflammatory attacks on organized religion in *The*

Age of Reason, published in 1794. Paine had been stewing about the subject for decades and, typically indifferent to the consequences, decided to pass along his conclusions.

The Age of Reason was a savage, witty and uncompromising attack on Christianity. Paine argued that the "worst-read-best-seller," the Bible, was not the word of God, and likened Christian beliefs to Greek mythology.

"I believe in one God and no more," he wrote. Among the things Paine did *not* believe: "the creed professed by the Jewish Church, by the Roman Church, by the Turkish Church, by the Protestant Church, nor by any church." All religious institutions, he added, were "human inventions, set up to terrify and enslave mankind, and monopolize power and profit." For good measure, Paine added that if God killed his only son, then He had broken the law.

Common Sense helped touch off the American Revolution; *The Rights of Man* electrified the reform movement in England and France. But with the publication of *The Age of Reason,* Paine set himself apart from other public heroes for good. His face would never appear on coins or bills; he'd never join the lineup of audioanimatronic patriots at Disney World. It was rumored that Washington and Jefferson shared Paine's views on religion, but neither was indiscreet enough ever to say so in public, let alone in print.

The counterattacks intensified. The American clergy was outraged. Several unfavorable biographies—one commissioned by the British government—portrayed Paine as an unkempt drunk and infidel. He soiled his bed rather than get up and use the outhouse, one writer "revealed." The aging revolutionary was frequently insulted on New York streets, where, even fully sober, he was often accused by passersby of being drunk.

The smear campaign provoked strikingly effective and long-lasting. For some time after his death, proposed statues of Paine couldn't be erected for fear of vandalism. On the one-hundredth anniversary of the Declaration of Independence, the city of Philadelphia refused to allow a bust of him to be displayed in Independence Hall. Theodore Roosevelt called him a "dirty little atheist." Paine's greatest gift may have been his ability to give voice to the frustrations and resentments of millions. As a result, he's often been dismissed as a demagogue or populist panderer. For decades, writes Claes, American historians relegated Paine to the sidelines of their revolution as a person of "marginal influence," if not dubious morality.

Worse, the ideals he embodied have vanished from the central consciousness of the mass media.

If heroism is defined as sticking to one's beliefs no matter what, however, Paine qualifies. His deathbed scene in Greenwich Village, after months of being moved from place to place in great pain, is described by Thomas Keane in his recent biography, *Tom Paine: A Political Life.*

Lapsing into unconsciousness, in agony from spreading and gangrenous bedsores, Paine woke occasionally to cry, "O Lord, help me! O Lord, help me!" Convinced that Paine's time on earth was nearly up, a physician and pastor named Manley "made the final attempt, using the combined powers of medicine and organized religion, to force his patient to recant." During one of Paine's last lucid moments, Manley slowly and deliberately said, "Allow me to ask again, Do you believe, or let me qualify the question, Do you wish to believe that Jesus Christ is the son of God?"

Incapable of compromise, even when it might have provided some comfort, Paine uttered his quiet last words: "I have no wish to believe on that subject."

"I know not whether any Man in the World has had more influence on its inhabitants or affairs for the last thirty years than Tom Paine," John Adams wrote to a friend after Paine's death, ". . . for such a mongrel between Pigg and Puppy, begotten by a wild Boar on a Bitch Wolf, never before in any Age of the World was suffered by the Poltroonery of mankind, to run through such a career of mischief. Call it then the Age of Paine."

It is not, in fact, called the Age of Paine. Paine's role in shaping his time is largely unknown to most Americans, even to many journalists whose work is made possible by his visions and sacrifices. In part, that's because the founder of journalism in America became one of its first major victims. "He did not see," writes Keane, "that he was among the first modern public figures to suffer firsthand an increasingly concentrated press equipped with the power to peddle one-sided interpretations of the world."

Unfortunately for Paine, wrote historian Crane Brinton in the *Saturday Review* (cited by Tommy Thompson in the *Midwest Quarterly* in 1991), revolutionaries need to die young or turn conservative in order not to lose favor with society. Paine did neither, and fell from grace. Many of his reform programs will always remain unacceptable to political conservatives, and his religious views will always offend believing Christians. Though his memory is invoked from time to time—during the Nazi threat, for instance—"his resurrection will never be complete," Thompson concludes.

Lately, though, his reputation is showing signs of at least some minor improvement. Officials in Washington have been considering a monument to him somewhere in the capital—though that was before Newt. And Sir Richard Attenborough, the famed British actor and director, has been struggling for several years to get studio backing for a film about Paine.

A Paine film biography could include lots of good Hollywood stuff—two bloody revolutions, a narrow escape from the guillotine, stand-offs with Napoleon, tangles with the House of Hanover, cameo roles for Washington, Jefferson, Robespierre and King George. It would make a socko miniseries, too.

Perhaps, after all that attention, somebody could even find Paine's bones.

✳

That they are missing may be the most fitting postscript to Paine's life. William Cobbett was a British journalist who wrote under the name "Peter Porcupine" and who hated Paine's ideas, even though he was a pamphleteer in the Paine tradition. But he had a change of heart. In his *Cobbett's Weekly Political Register*, Cobbett, smarting at the way Paine had been treated in his final years, wrote: "Paine lies in a little hole under the grass and weeds of an obscure farm in America. There, however, he shall not lie, unnoticed, much longer. He belongs to England."

Just before dawn one autumn night in 1818, Cobbett, his son and a friend went to Paine's New Rochelle farm, where his remains were buried. (Today the "hole under the grass" is marked by a plaque on the grounds of the Thomas Paine Historical Society.) They dug up his grave, determined that Paine should have a proper burial in his native country. After that the story grows fuzzy. By most accounts, Cobbett fled with Paine's bones to New York City, pursued by a local sheriff, who gave chase too late. Cobbett never publicly buried the remains, and some historians think he lost them overboard on the return voyage. But some British newspapers reported that they were displayed in November 1819 in Liverpool.

After Cobbett's death in 1835, his son auctioned off all his worldly goods. Paine's bones weren't among them. Some reports say they were secretly buried on the Cobbett family property. In 1854, however, a Unitarian minister in England claimed to own Paine's skull and right hand (though he wouldn't show them to anybody). Parts of Paine, truly by now the "universal citizen" he wanted to be, have been reported turning up intermittently ever since. In the 1930s, a woman in Brighton claimed to own what clearly would be the best part of Paine to have—his jawbone. Historian Moncure Daniel Conway wrote a hundred years ago: "As to his bones, no man knows the place of their rest to this day. His principles rest not."

❋

His principles, in fact, are demonstrated daily in the opinionated anarchy of the Net, created in part by misfits and outsiders whose vision of liberated information would sound awfully familiar to Paine. In a way, he created it too.

It's easy to imagine him fitting right into the new culture, issuing fervent harangues from http://www.commonsense.com. He would be a cyber provocateur, a Net fiend, perpetually enmeshed in bitter disputes with adversaries in government, corporations, churches.

Picture him logging on from the still-standing small brown wooden cottage on his New Rochelle farm—the one given him by New York State in appreciation for his services during the Revolution. He'd sit at his desktop computer by the stone fireplace with a steaming bowl of soup, utterly addicted. Technologically challenged, never into mechanical details, Paine would have an older Macintosh he'd be extremely loath to replace.

He would belong to contentious conferencing systems like the WELL or New York's Echo, but he would especially love cruising the more populist big boards— Prodigy, CompuServe, AOL. He would check the Netizen's message boards and tear into Republicans and Democrats daily. He would send the *New England Journal of Medicine* his tracts on the spread of disease, and pepper *Scientific American* with his ideas about bridges. His would put up his own Web site and make it a world center for hell-raising and reasoned argument. He would bombard Congress with e-mail and the White House Internet site with proposals, reforms and legislative initiatives, tackling the most explosive subjects, never tiptoeing around but attacking them head-on, enraging, at one time or another, everybody.

The Net would help enormously in his various campaigns, allowing him to call up research papers, download his latest tract, fire off hundreds of angry posts and receive hundreds of replies.

They would hear from him soon enough in China and Iran, Croatia and Burundi. He would not be happy to find the descendants of his old nemeses from the House of Hanover still around in Britain, but would be amused to see George's heirs reduced to tabloid fodder and relieved to find France a republic after all. As radical as he would be, he would not like the Politically Correct, and would provoke and enrage them continuously as inhibitors of free speech. He would emit nuclear flames from time to time; their targets would emerge singed and sooty. He would not use smileys.

He would be spared the excruciating loneliness he faced in later life on that modest farm, where neighbors shunned him and visitors rarely came. Thanks to the Net, he would no longer be an outcast but would find at least as many kindred spirits as adversaries, his cyber-mailbox eternally full. Unlike almost any other medium, Net culture is filled with stories of rescues, aid efforts and assistance for the stranded, the ill and the despairing. Think how it would have risen to Paine's need.

He would appreciate his online community, since he might not find much friendship from other journalists. He would hate Manhattan media movers and shun them like the plague. He would hate Washington reporters even more and would be enraged to learn that some take big fees to speak to trade associations and to participate in mock impassioned discussions on

television, and that they court politicians and one another at pricey restaurants and on golf courses.

Paine would greatly prefer the computer to the cock-
tail party. His notions of spare, direct writing would
work beautifully on the Net, enriching it and permit-
ting him to be productive and to address an audience
even after his gout made traveling difficult. He would
find himself, in fact, smack in the center of his greatest
dream, a member of a "universal society, whose mind
rises above the atmosphere of local thoughts and con-
siders mankind, of whatever nation or profession they
may be, as the work of one Creator."

If life would be easier for him, it would not be easy.
Intense personal relationships would still elude him.
Like at least some of his Net successors, he did not
have substantial social skills. He would still be reclu-
sive and moody, too obnoxious and combative to have
dinner with Bill and Hillary, to be lionized by academe
or hired by major media outlets. Worse, the country
still isn't ready for most of his ideas. Up to a certain
point, radicalism can be lucrative in America, but
Paine would refuse book deals from Rupert Murdoch
and flee in horror at offers from Washington talk
shows. He would probably find most newspapers un-
bearably tepid and write angry letters to editors, canceling his subscription.

He and the massing corporate entities drooling over
the Net would be instantly and ferociously at war as he
recognized Time Warner, TCI, the Baby Bells and Viacom as different incarnations of the same elements
that scarfed up the press and homogenized it. His battle cries would be aimed at keeping all the junk they're

selling off the Net, at keeping access to it cheap and open enough for individuals. He'd have lots to say about the so-called information highway and the government's alleged role in shaping it. One of his pamphlets—this might be the only thing he'd have in common with Newt Gingrich—would surely propose means of getting more computers and modems into the hands of people who can't afford them.

Instead of dying alone and in agony, Paine would spend his last days sending poignant e-mail all over the world, via a Powerbook in his sickbed. He'd journal online about the shortcomings of medicine and the mystical experience of aging while digging into his inexhaustible supply of prescriptions for eradicating the incalculable injustices that still afflict the world.

Chapter 8

MEDIA NOW: THE SIMPSON TRIAL

Information wants to be free, the Internet slogan goes. By the same token, media want to tell the truth. That neither force gets what it wants much of the time is one of the great ironic dramas of the information revolution.

But if you watch those screens and read enough, carefully enough, for long enough, the truth unfailingly struggles to break through, often in indirect and surprising ways.

In the O. J. Simpson trial, the truth revealed was this: The country and some of its most important institutions have become mired in a mean-spirited standoff between factions whose primary characteristic is self-righteous obstinacy. Our open spaces—courts, workplaces, Congress, academe—are no longer meeting places but are battlegrounds on which the most pressing struggles never get resolved. We are no longer one nation, if we ever were; we are a landmass peopled by many bitterly divided tribes. Wherever we come together to thrash out common values, laws and understandings, we can't.

And the institution most responsible for spotting this big story and helping us to come to terms with it doesn't do its job. The power of modern media is a great hoax, exposed by Orenthal James Simpson and the spectacle he provoked in Los Angeles in 1995.

If this was one of our most interesting stories ever, it was also one of our most brutal. The trial brought to mainstream America overpowering evidence of this new reality: The notion of one nation united by common views of attainable equality, justice and individual freedom is a myth. Day after day, some of our most cherished social beliefs were chipped away, witness by witness. The police didn't stand for justice, which is clearly not the least bit blind; the lawyers didn't represent the law; the jury couldn't promise unbiased judgment; the judge didn't ensure order and journalism didn't supply the truth.

Our society had no mechanism to try O. J. Simpson rationally in those circumstances at that time. It can't deal with paralyzing social tensions; it seeks to curb technology it can't control; it virtually guarantees that informed, fair-minded people be barred from the jury system.

No institution in this spectacle seemed more bankrupt than the media themselves. Technology allowed them to bring us the words and pictures more quickly and clearly than ever, but they had lost the will to explain what those images meant. The media don't help

us to talk to or comprehend one another; they simply
encourage us to state our differences ever more stri-
dently. The people working for them are not prepared
or permitted to acknowledge the way the enormous social, ethnic and political changes transforming our culture permeated the story unfolding in front of them.

On the scary road to Simpsonville, some of our most
central institutions seemed nearly overwhelmed.

"FRAGMENTED IDENTITIES"

There were more reporters gathered around the O. J.
Simpson trial for longer periods, generating more
words and videotape, than gathered around any other
domestic story ever. Mostly, they presented the trial as
a sort of ethnocentric Super Bowl, offering a daily tip-
sheet and scorecard: when criminalist Fung faltered, it
was good for the defense; the DNA evidence proved a
"victory" for the prosecution. One legal strategy was
checkmated by another; defense against prosecution,
journalists against jurists, experts against experts, jurors against jurors, whites against blacks. The coverage
provided staggering amounts of sometimes useful but
often banal play-by-play.

As it turns out, the big story at the O. J. Simpson
trial didn't have much to do with blood droplets or police bungling. The story is even more troubling than
murder.

Though we pretend that everybody is alike and equal
and approaches our common civic work with the same

basic values, the images flickering across millions of TVs clearly showed the polarization of American life. America is increasingly a collection of tribal enclaves, each responsive to its own interests and unable or unwilling to step beyond itself on behalf of a common good. Journalists are one of the many tribes in LA, whites another, African-Americans another, as are the police, defense attorneys, prosecutors and jurors.

And each tribe has unyielding agendas that conflict expensively and interminably with the others. Costly lawyers and batteries of experts battled the plodding investigative bureaucracy to near-collapse, subjecting low-level clerks to days of relentless battering and even the pettiest evidential procedures to intense scrutiny.

The trial reinforced the idea that America is a country of divisions, not all of them racial. Gender and other social fractures also were reflected in the coverage.

If more anthropologists could write, a lot of journalists would have to find work. And if journalists were given the time, education and training anthropologists have, we might better grasp some of the complicated problems we face.

There are, writes anthropologist Arjun Appadurai in a chapter of *Recapturing Anthropology: Working in the Present,* some "brute facts" for modern anthropologists to confront. For the rest of us, too.

Central among them, says Appadurai, "is the changing social, territorial, and cultural reproduction of group identity. As groups migrate, regroup in new locations, reconstruct their histories, and reconfigure their ethnic 'projects' " or goals, the "landscapes of group identity" all over the world are changing.

Appadurai calls these new communities "ethno-scapes" and notes that they seem to be sprouting all over the United States. One important source of this change, he writes, is the mass media, which present a rich and constantly changing gallery of possibilities. Mobility, diversity and media exposure alter groups' expectations, generate instability, cement differences, exacerbate conflict.

Thus, historically impoverished or oppressed people "no longer see their lives as mere outcomes of the givenness of things." Instead of accepting their fates, they retain their own values and reject many of those imposed by the cultures they find themselves in.

All over the planet, definitions of what nations are and mean are changing, a big story in anthropology if not on our evening newscasts or front pages. "We live in a . . . world of crisscrossed economies, intersecting systems of meaning, and fragmented identities," writes Roger Rouse in *Diaspora,* a journal of transnational studies. We have moved, he cautions, into a new kind of social space.

One prototype for this new kind of space could well be Simpsonville. If these analysts are correct, we may have to step back from Los Angeles a lot farther to come to terms with what we're seeing.

In days to come, says essayist Barbara Ehrenreich in *The Snarling Citizen,* she'll explain to the grandkids asking about the Simpson trial that "we were starved for any sort of tribal experience. We lived each shut up in our single-family homes, yearning for an outbreak of communal drumming and dancing or perhaps a spectacular blood sacrifice." Whatever we yearn for, what we seem to be getting is a culture losing any sense of commonality.

The media are telling us this truth, sort of—they just don't know that they are. You can see it in every local paper, commercial newscast and CNN hourly report. From the Capitol to town halls, our media depict a quagmire. We seem stuck in a public tar pit over every issue that counts: the environment, education, budgets, poverty, gender, culture and race. The media themselves are divided, one element accusing the other of promoting sensationalism and dumbing-down. This is a new politics of entrenchment, whereby sides dig in and fight for every bloody inch of ground and where the function of media is to transmit pictures and quotes of people shouting at one another.

(AT LEAST) TWO NATIONS

By far the most jarring of these divisions, as the Simpson story repeatedly demonstrated, is the racial one. Sometime during the trial, it became clear to most white Americans that O. J. Simpson was probably guilty, that the DNA and other evidence was substantial, that the idea of a massive police conspiracy to frame him was ludicrous, at best a desperate play by high-powered lawyers. Almost at the same time, it became equally clear to most African-Americans that Simpson was probably innocent, and that a police conspiracy was not only possible but likely. It also became clear to both groups that the Simpson jury was probably not going to convict him.

Newsweek pollsters found that only 11 percent of nonwhite Americans would have voted guilty as of mid-April, as opposed to 49 percent of whites. An earlier *Newsweek* poll had found that 60 percent of blacks believed Simpson was set up by the police or "other forces." The numbers fluctuated somewhat, but throughout the trial polls consistently suggested that nearly 70 percent of whites were leaning toward believing Simpson guilty, while the overwhelming majority of blacks felt he was innocent.

Sociologist Andrew Hacker described America this way in the title of his landmark work: *Two Nations, Black and White, Separate, Hostile, Unequal.* That could as easily have been the theme of the Simpson trial. America is inherently a white country, writes Hacker, while blacks face boundaries and restrictions set by the white majority.

Though many white Americans want to view racism as an ugly part of America's past, African-Americans see it as part of their daily reality. White Americans' expectations of blacks—that they move happily and quickly into the mainstream as a result of their new educational and economic opportunities—have never been higher, while many blacks' expectations of their own prospects plunge.

"A huge racial chasm remains, and there are few signs that the coming century will see it closed," writes Hacker. "A century and a quarter after slavery white America continues to ask of its black citizens an extra patience and perseverance that whites have never required of themselves."

Simpsonville, our national headquarters for fragmentation and imploding institutions, suggested that it may no longer be possible to do business or come to resolution in common settings like courtrooms.

If whites were puzzled by black anger, they didn't have to be. There's lots of terrific reporting about it outside of mainstream media, in works like Hacker's or in Christopher Jencks's *Rethinking Social Policy: Race, Poverty and the Underclass.* NYU law professor Derrick Bell argues in *Faces at the Bottom of the Well* that racism is so endemic in American life that blacks need to give up on the idea of overcoming it and concentrate instead on surviving it. Writers like Ellis Cose detail the epidemic anger even among the most successful, "assimilated" black Americans. Philosopher Cornel West writes frequently of a "sheer failure of nerve" of liberals and journalists who hesitate to risk real discussion of racial issues.

The bleak and powerful writing of these scholars hardly makes the black-white schism surrounding the Simpson trial easier to take, but it moves the discussion past knee-jerk responses that stifle real comprehension or progress. It becomes much clearer why white and black jurors can look at the very same people saying the same things and reach totally different conclusions.

This is perhaps the heart not only of the Simpson story but of the media's failure to cover this trial incisively: they lacked the ability to be blunt enough, deep enough or analytical enough to help us understand not just what we were seeing but why. What the anthropologists are telling us is what journalists should be writing about—the way entrenched social problems, mobility, technology, immigration and the break-up of empires and superpowers are knocking us off our civic pins.

In the days after the Oklahoma bombing, for instance, it became clear that "heartland" clichés no longer applied. We learned, slowly, that Oklahoma City—a name nearly synonymous with white, semi-rural, Christian America—is home to substantial numbers of Muslims, African-Americans, Asians, Mexicans and Eastern Europeans, many of whom resist incorporation into a national identity.

Certain historians, anthropologists and social scientists seem to have known about the fragmentation of America for years. In a stream of compelling literature, they've pointed out that politicians are locked in eternally warring camps, stalemating the political process with their refusal to compromise or reach beyond narrow constituencies. And that blacks and whites and Asians and Hispanics are hopelessly divided on a widening range of social and civic issues. Authors have described a culture of victimization, complaint and rage permeating almost every part of American life. But because our mass media shy away from such indictments, we don't have to acknowledge their sobering truth or do anything about them.

One reason for the jarring cultural clashes between new and old media is that the visions of America that they put forth are so fundamentally different. Through the early 1960s, the usual presentation of America was an Eisenhower-ish one: Women stayed at home while prosperous males conducted the country's business. Minorities were largely invisible. Justice and opportunity prevailed. We had no idea how many unhappy women, gays, blacks, Hispanics, there were because no-body asked them how they felt, or much cared. (Now that we claim to care, we have to listen to all the vitriol.)

New media present a strikingly different portrait. Spike Lee's efforts to provoke discussion about racism in movies like *Do the Right Thing* are heroic, writes author Michael Eric Dyson; they expose "a stunning loss of conscience about race." Other cultural institutions—like journalism—haven't been as courageous.

Historian Benjamin Schwarz put it bluntly in *The Atlantic Monthly:* "Through most of America's history the nation's unity and stability have derived not from a welcome of diversity but from imposition of the dominant Anglo culture." The so-called "unity" of the American people, writes Schwarz, was due to the ability of an "Anglo elite" to stamp its image on newcomers.

But that unity no longer prevails. For better or worse, Schwarz says, the current fragmentation and "direction-lessness" of American society are the result, above all, of the disintegrating elite's inability or unwillingness to impose its values. Nowhere does this seem more true than in Simpsonville, where a host of competing interests and cultural experiences collided in American living rooms.

THE FAILED CULT OF OBJECTIVITY

On high school newspapers, in university journalism schools, among young reporters entering daily journalism, objectivity is taught as the professional standard—along with accuracy—to which journalists aspire. Most working journalists, especially older ones, accept it as bedrock: they aim to be detached and impartial, setting aside personal political or emotional beliefs.

Many people, inside and outside journalism, believe that complete objectivity is not an attainable goal for most human beings. "Nevertheless, we can still distinguish personal attitudes, religious dogmas, and the like from facts and justified beliefs," write Georgetown professors Stephen Klaidman and Tom L. Beauchamp in *The Virtuous Journalist.* "The essence of some professional commitments is engagement, but in contrast to adherents of the so-called new journalism, we believe . . . that journalists are obligated to maintain a professional distance."

This ethic not only requires the impossible but makes viewers' and readers' tasks difficult. Since they know the total absence of bias isn't possible in most human beings, they have to guess to what degree journalists are influenced by personal beliefs, and they frequently assume the worst: that journalists' offerings flow from personal prejudice. Even when they make arguments openly and support them, journalists are suspected of advancing secret agendas and are rendered less, not more, credible. Commentators like Rush Limbaugh may be widely disliked, but they attract vast followings because they are unfailingly outspoken, not "objective."

The nature of modern politics has altered the meaning of detachment as well. To the gay person seeking a government response to AIDS, or to an underclass mother whose family is engulfed by drugs and guns, a disinterested attitude about such life-and-death issues constitutes a hostile act. Such people, turning to media that choose to be detached about their problems, will soon find other media.

So, too, with the young, flocking to media that they perceive as much more truthful than the mainstream press, that offer strong points of view, frank exchanges of ideas, graphic visual presentations and lots of irony and self-deprecating humor.

Still, the idea that reporters must suppress their views and perceptions remains deeply ingrained. "I wouldn't dare write what I think," a reporter who helped cover the Simpson case for the *Los Angeles Times* told a San Francisco graduate journalism seminar. What the reporter thought was that Simpson was guilty and that the jury would never convict him, mostly for racial reasons. "I'll be frank," a senior editor at *Time,* also afraid to be publicly identified, confided in e-mail. "We'd get massacred if we printed what our reporters think. I know it sounds weird, but it's true. We just could never get away with it." It is strange and true—and chilling—that an institution founded on free and fearless speech doesn't dare speak freely.

(Since we're on the subject, here's what I believe: In light of the evidence presented at trial, O. J. Simpson seemed to me profoundly disturbed. I believe he was guilty of killing Nicole Simpson and Ronald Goldman. I also believed and wrote that he would not be convicted, primarily because of racial tensions in Los Angeles and because the legal system has no sane mechanism for selecting a jury able to cope with the social pressures and legal complexities of such trials.)

Decades back, when newspapers were homogeneous in their politics and marketing—published by white men for white men about white men—objectivity worked in both the marketing and journalistic sense. Papers became so respectable and inoffensive that they were able to amass large audiences; with little competition, they monopolized news and advertising from the mid-nineteenth century to the 1960s.

But as the nation became more diverse, and as new journalism technology provided fierce competition, objectivity paralyzed more than it professionalized. And as a result of TV, cable, VCRs, computers and modems, the young now have a vast new culture to turn to, not only for new kinds of advertising (i.e., music videos) but for the outspoken opinion, vivid writing, visual imagery, and informality they prefer. Ascending media— from rapidly proliferating home pages to programs by Comedy Central—make no pretense of being "objective," comprehensive or even substantial.

Among modern journalists a handful—the late Randy Shilts comes most readily to mind—have rejected objectivity. Shilts's book *And the Band Played On* remains the most powerful and definitive history of the AIDS epidemic in America, fusing passion and fact into a kind of journalism that values truth-telling above balance. But such examples are rare.

Proponents of objectivity argue that its loss would lead to a chorus of shrill, confusing voices further obscuring the truth. But journalists are apt to be less shrill and more even-handed than many of the people they quote and videotape. Journalism can continue to preach reverence for informed opinion based on research, accuracy and fairness while allowing writers and reporters to tell the truth as they see it.

Nor is objectivity the only chilling factor. The demand for "politically correct" speech has drastically curbed open discussion of race and gender. The unguarded, dumb or insensitive remark, followed by profuse apology, has become one of our sadder public spectacles, destroying careers and reputations. It is safer to avoid sensitive subjects. Only talk-show hosts or right-wing radio and TV commentators seem free to say what they think.

If Benjamin Schwarz or Arjun Appadurai could have anchored some of the coverage out of LA, with field commentary from sociologists, historians and writers like Hacker, Jencks, Ehrenreich, Wendy Kaminer, Henry Louis Gates, Jr., or Elijah Anderson, we might better have understood some of the forces that brought us to the mess in LA. The problem with media coverage of the Simpson trial wasn't that there was too much of it, but that there was too little of the right sort.

What would subjective news media look like?

They would follow the model Randy Shilts set: strong point of view, intense sense of social justice, reverence for facts, determination to tell the truth.

In the case of the Simpson story, journalists would have reported not only on the trial but on the racial climate in Los Angeles, the economics of justice, the overwhelming impact of media and the glaring inadequacies of the jury system. They would have presented the trial's daily developments, but they would have been free—encouraged, in fact—to state their opinions, as long as they were supported by facts and strong reasoning, and to change their minds and explain why: "Today, I came to believe O. J. Simpson was innocent, and here's the evidence that made me think so."

COURTROOM MELTDOWN

The Simpson trial, as it wound on, caused a loss of faith. An American Bar Association poll in the spring of 1995 found that 45 percent of those surveyed said the trial caused them to lose respect for the justice system. Only 28 percent of the people questioned by ABA pollsters the previous July had given that response.

Like journalism, the legal profession waxes effusive about love of law, constitutional guarantees, passion for justice. This was hardly the picture that emerged from the bickering, posturing and maneuvering in Los Angeles. It seemed clear that the criminal justice system could be overwhelmed by large infusions of money, influenced by mass concentrations of media and paralyzed by racial divisions.

In his best-selling and controversial book *The Death of Common Sense,* attorney Philip K. Howard painted a frightening portrait of a legal system no longer under anyone's control. Howard's examples have been challenged by journalists and lawyers, yet many of his premises ring true. In an observation that perfectly fits the loony twists and turns of the Simpson trial, Howard wrote that "law makes us feel like its victims. We divert our energies into defensive measures designed solely to avoid tripping over rules that seem to exist only because someone put them there."

Take the court's oddly ambivalent attitude toward media. Cultural isolation might have been possible when news consisted of a daily paper, a weekly magazine or an evening newscast. But news channels are on television twenty-four hours a day now, and there are nearly a thousand radio talk shows. Fax machines, cell phones, satellites, modems and computers and Web pages have made information ubiquitous. There is no way to isolate a potential juror or anybody else from the pervasive media and their messages. Nor is there any reason to. Either jurors are forced to pretend they live in cocoons, or they really do live in cocoons and are poorly prepared for their role of deciding enormously complex issues.

The more you know about the law in general, says author Wendy Kaminer, or about a case in particular, the less likely you are to wind up on a jury. Litigators, she points out, don't seek objective, unbiased jurors but look for biased ones—people who they believe favor their side of the case. And, she adds, concern about pretrial publicity favors uninformed over informed jurors.

As the drama of the Simpson jury demonstrated, a jury no longer does what it was meant to do—function as the true conscience of the community—but represents only those parts of the community, those tribes, to which individual jurors belong. Ex-juror Jeanette Harris made this contradiction clear, shocking many whites, when she told reporters in mid-trial that she believed none of the evidence presented against

Simpson and pointed out that jurors could hardly be expected to transcend racial issues, since whites and blacks had to go back and live in their own communities afterward. If she had made those views clear at the outset, she would probably never have gotten on the jury.

Whether they realized it or not, reporters covering the trial seemed to have abandoned even the pretense that jurors could transcend racial issues. Jurors were routinely identified by race, and it was virtually assumed that the loss of an African-American juror amounted to a setback for the defense and the loss of a white or Hispanic a defeat for the prosecution. If the reporters were right—and the speed of the "deliberation" before the verdict seemed to show that they were—then the jury system is clearly unworkable in racially charged cases. If they were wrong, then they advanced the worst kind of stereotypes.

In *With Justice for Some: Victims' Rights in Criminal Trials,* Professor George P. Fletcher of the Columbia University Law School makes a number of specific, logical recommendations for reforming the courts, including changes in the selection of juries. In the era of CNN and Court TV, Fletcher writes, high-profile cases cannot escape the notice of even the most remote citizens. Jurors should be screened not to find the ignorant or ill informed but to find those "capable of maintaining an open mind until they hear the evidence presented at trial." Fletcher and other legal scholars point out that, historically, the motive in jury selection wasn't to pick detached citizens but to choose peers of the accused who were *part of* his or her community and could act on its behalf. People cut off from the free flow of information, locked in motels for months while being spied on by deputies, seem far from that ideal.

In modern America, it might be feasible to consider empaneling jurors willing to acknowledge and discuss racial perceptions and biases, instead of forcing them to pretend they have none. Fletcher calls for the establishment of an "interactive jury," an idea that would have looked pretty good in the Simpson case. "As they now function," he writes, "jury trials display little capacity for self-correction and avoidance of irrational tangents." Rather than sequestering jurors, he argues, judges should encourage outside-the-courtroom contacts, inviting jurors to submit written questions to the judge throughout the trial in order to understand the law.

Although Fletcher doesn't suggest it, it would also make sense to encourage jurors to read and see lots of different media and discuss them, perhaps with the judge and attorneys. In the Simpson case, wouldn't it have been healthier for white jurors to read African-American newspapers and magazines like the *Chicago Crusader,* which wrote in an editorial that "white men have a deep abiding fear that black men will take their women from them"? Likewise, if juror Harris had been permitted to read some of the mainstream media coverage, she might have wondered more about how Nicole Simpson's blood wound up on her ex-husband's socks and have fretted less over how O.J. was bearing up under all the pressure.

Judges seem to react to media the same way boomer parents do: rather than struggle with how best to use modern media and their attendant technologies, they find it easier to ban them.

DIGITAL NEWS

New media were also paying attention to the trial. Time Warner's Pathfinder site on the Web had an active Simpson conference, as did the WELL's media and current-events conferences, AOL, Prodigy, Court TV and other sites and newsgroups. One Web site was a virtual directory to all things Simpson on the Net: http://www.yahoo.com/Law/Cases/OJ_Simpson_Case/. The site guided trial watchers to Cyber Sight's O.J. poll, humor topics, Simpson products like court transcripts—and to news: alt.fan.ojsimpson, a well-organized, useful and sometimes quite provocative series offering information and discussions about everything from DNA to the collection of blood evidence.

But although individual discussion is much freer online than off, online news has yet to become influential or to grasp or exploit its own potential. It hasn't defined its own ethic or function in covering stories like O. J. Simpson.

Journalistically, its biggest breakthrough is returning individuals to stories like this, giving them a chance to bypass journalists and ask questions, express themselves, share concerns. But with so many voices speaking at once, it's difficult for most people to find the ones they most want or need to hear.

Meanwhile, the big boards are content to rent space to mainstream media rather than present themselves as distinct editorial entities willing to use new media in new ways. And the traditional news media pouring on-line bring their usual timidity to digital coverage; happy to let users mouth off in forums and via e-mail, they remain as cautious online as they are on their editorial pages.

Yet the possibilities are exciting. AOL or Prodigy could easily set up national black-white racial forums in which individuals could speak frankly about race, ask one another questions, begin a dialogue in a medium that permits users to encounter people they would otherwise never meet. Blacks could talk about their perceptions of racism and justice; white males could talk about their fear of displacement; scholars like Jencks or West could come online to answer questions and share their research findings. People of different races, genders and sexual orientations could forge links. Every online user knows that this kind of communicating often breaks down barriers, forcing sender and receiver to deal with one another as individuals rather than as group members.

There is already precedent: During the debate over gays in the military, gay soldiers spoke directly to wary veterans on CompuServe. There are nearly a dozen newsgroups for African-American professionals on the Net, several for police officers who have shot people or been shot, one for black cops struggling to reconcile racial history with police work. Online news suggests a forum in which it would be easier for fragmented political or racial groups to begin what will be a tortuous process: teaching the members of all those tribes how to communicate with one another, and providing them with a simple means of doing so.

It will happen during some future big story. Some of the big online services are already creating digital newsrooms, hiring editorial staff and experimenting with ways to respond to events like the Oklahoma City bombing. All during the 1996 election, online services were reporting up-to-the-minute poll and election results, announcements and campaign news.

For better or worse, great stories have always transformed the media that cover them. Walter Cronkite's coverage of the Kennedy assassination and the moon landing were broadcast journalism's twin high-water marks, legitimizing TV news as the country's most pervasive news medium. Watergate brought the press into its ongoing age of antagonism and self-righteousness. The death of Elvis Presley sparked a booming new tabloid news culture that's become a permanent part of our information structure. The Gulf War and CNN's coverage of it made cable television the country's premier medium for breaking news.

But in 1995 came one of the biggest stories of modern times, the one people told pollsters they were tired of hearing about and then rushed to watch and talk about.

The Simpson trial transformed people's information habits, pulling enormous numbers of viewers and readers away from papers, newscasts, soap operas and talk shows.

Mid-trial, an astonishing forty million people—24 percent of the adult public—said they were watching all or most of the live coverage. An even larger num-ber—59 percent—said they had watched, read or heard some news about the trial the day before the sur-vey interview. The most-dedicated Simpson watchers, according to a Times Mirror Center survey, were twice as likely as moderate O.J. followers to tune in to CNN and three times as likely to use Court TV.

For the first time in a generation, all our media were covering the same thing: *New York Times* reporters side by side with the *National Enquirer*'s, *CBS News* bump-ing up against *Inside Edition*. Even a story as big as the Gulf War attracted primarily traditional, not new, media; conversely the mainstream press held its nose through the Amy Fisher saga and Tonya-and-Nancy, happy to leave them mostly to the tabs. Not this time. The Simpson story blurred the boundaries.

This was not, as some journalism professors and pun-dits suggested, the end of civilization. The straight press learned that it's okay to be interesting once in a while, and the tabloids became less shrill and irresponsible. Writing in the *Columbia Journalism Review, Time* mag-azine law reporter Andrea Sachs noted that many jour-nalists regularly read the trial coverage of the *National Enquirer,* which had won "grudging respect from its mainstream rivals for the thoroughness and accuracy, if not always the taste and fairness, of its coverage."

Mainstream media pundits hated the trial, of course, as they have come to loathe almost any story Americans love to watch and see. They scolded their own col-leagues for covering it so much and the rest of us for watching it so much. But nobody had any reason to feel guilty about following this trial.

It usually takes only one or two compelling elements to drive the biggest stories. With murder, mystery, race, gender, class, wealth, celebrity, abuse, sports, cops, criminal justice, the rise and fall of a hero, this one had nearly every element there is. It told us much about ourselves.

Chapter 9

LOOKING FORWARD

MEDIA DINOSAURS: ADAPT OR DIE

A word to the old-style media, as they cling to the cliff with stiffening fingers:

Your Web sites and online newspapers won't save you. But there is a place for traditional news media, if you'll take a breather from the culture wars and do some hard thinking about change. It will be difficult, but it may mean survival.

CLIP 'N' SAVE

■ Play to your strengths, not your weaknesses. Reading newspapers online, for example, is like watching Lawrence Welk try to rap. It doesn't work.

Online services offer no context, no sense of place, no distinctive voices. They are about free-form expression, community building, business communications and, in certain corners, about art and creativity. It's not bad for you that they're sprouting all over the place. The more of them there are, the more distinctive and valuable you can appear, by providing coherence, rationality and context.

Online services and the Web have significant limitations. Digital culture is, at this point in its adolescence, fragmented, confusing, expensive and time-consuming. Its very uncensored nature makes it a fine forum for ideas, but less reliable as a credible arbiter and analyst. We can hear what everybody is saying online, but we often don't know what to make of it. The press, with its historic and familiar role in our daily lives, culture and politics, can present issues clearly, factually, to large numbers of people at once.

But newspapers will have to drop the pretense that they are passing along actual news. Cable and digital technology have completely coopted the dissemination of breaking news stories. No medium that prints or broadcasts several times a day can possibly compete with a medium that is always available. So don't try to do what such rivals invariably do better. Do what they do poorly: investigative reporting, documentaries, special reports, longer interviews, analysis. Sift, provide context, sort through the mess every day; help us decide what we need to pay attention to.

Much as we like to kick you around, you're important. The good news is that we need you. The bad news is that you will have to change more than you have been willing to, though not as much as you fear. You won't have to compromise your values and standards.

In fact, just the opposite: you'll have to reaffirm those that you began with.

■ Lighten up. This may be the hardest part—take yourself less seriously. Drop the harrumphing, tut-tutting voice. Stop presuming you have a lock on wisdom and justice. You're not smarter than anybody else, you just control more machinery.

Interactive media are informal, ironic, self-mocking, conversational. They don't lecture. They aren't afraid of arguments. To coexist with them, you'll have to deflate some.

■ Call off the war on kids. Refrain from suggesting that kids are stupid and helpless; stop attacking the culture and technology that are central to their lives. Historically, you've lost every one of these fights, from comics to rock and roll, on to rap and computers; each time, you just appear dumber, more out of it, and less relevant. Accept that the moral (and mortal) danger isn't to middle-class children watching MTV or playing with computers; that the most pressing values issue isn't that some people have too much technology, but that so many don't have any.

Kids are your lifeblood and future livelihood. They hate you, and who can blame them? Would you use a medium that continually branded you dumb and violent, that crapped on everything you love? By far the worst crisis the press faces is that the young think you lie about almost everything of value in their lives. They think you're out of it, prone to distorting and exaggerating dangers, clueless about the content and purpose of their culture. American kids now have the most diverse, sophisticated and interesting culture on the planet. They aren't going to give it up. Grasp this or pass into history.

If you want to be useful, cover technology and new media well. Help kids figure out how to access and keep up with them.

While you're at it, hire some young reporters, writers and editors. More young people get medical degrees every year than land jobs on big daily newspapers. Middle-aged and older reporters are great assets, knowledgeable, careful, experienced. But if we've learned anything in the past generation, it's that they can't cover the information revolution intelligently. They don't have time to trawl the Web or scan several dozen cable channels, and they don't "get" Larry King. They need help from their juniors.

■ Tell the truth about social problems and political issues. Stop hiding behind objectivity and "balance," quoting professional spokespeople and lobbyists; talk less to pollsters and more to us. If minority kids are responsible for most of the escalation in violence in recent years, tell us so and tell us why. If you think O.J. is guilty, say so and explain. If certain dangers and problems—campus rape, child abduction, homelessness—have been exaggerated, say so. Tell us on the front page. Raise at least as much hell about gun trafficking as you do about violent Hollywood films. Fight the constraints of political correctness, anathema to a medium that needs to make itself invaluable by speaking factually, clearly and passionately about issues.

■ Looks count. Hire some knockout designers.

Newspapers need desperately to do what some magazines have done—signal clearly that they are changing, not with the occasional color picture but with radical redesign. They need new logos, new fonts and type displays, new ways to use photos, animation, artwork and charts, different ways to present information. Ditto for network news, which needs to stop blowing millions on anchors' salaries and experiment with formats, sets and styles.

Magazines, MTV and Web designers have redefined graphic presentation. Picking up on their innovations is a powerful subliminal and explicit signal that you get it.

■ Vastly expand coverage of popular culture. In America, culture, politics and media have become indistinguishable. We are what we read, see and listen to. Every supposedly political issue in America flows through popular culture. *Thelma and Louise* foreshadowed Anita Hill. Bruce Springsteen broke the news that good jobs weren't easy to find anymore. *The X-Files* taps into our ambivalence about government power and morality. Snoop Doggy Dogg and his gangsta colleagues rub our noses in racial hatred and misogyny even when we'd much prefer to forget they exist.

Popular culture is universal. Americans may fight bitterly about guns or abortion, but they are all familiar with the medical dramas on *ER,* and first thing Monday morning they are waiting to trade reviews of the weekend's movies. Pop culture doesn't supplant serious news, it absorbs and incorporates it. It's a huge story; cover it.

■ Get interactive. Interactivity is a powerful idea, interesting, democratizing and extraordinarily popular.

Every major story in every paper should include an e-mail address, so that readers can react instantly, offering reporters criticism, praise, and other kinds of feedback. Reporters should respond to every sane and civil reader. Replace letters-to-the-editor pages with whole sections of reader feedback and debate. Eliminate op-ed pages, which have served to ghettoize commentary and make the most important issues we face seem tepid and stalemated. Encourage readers to report and contribute stories and opinion pieces, along with the usual academics and lobbyists.

Most important, editors, reporters and producers need to begin thinking interactively—a distinctly different state of mind, requiring years, perhaps decades, of new hiring, retraining and reorienting. Familiar to any person online for an hour, interactivity involves a profound readjustment.

Publication of the story is no longer the end of the editorial process; it's the beginning. Your mistakes will be pointed out, sometimes impolitely. People better informed than you will tell you what else you should have included; they'll often be right. Cranks will call you names—but people will also have the means to praise you instantly, which can be very nice, and to pass along story ideas, tips and valuable information.

The bottom line is that interactivity has political implications: It requires the people with all the power to accept less, while the people with none of the power acquire some. This seems to be the toughest task by far: inducing journalists to relinquish the idea that they alone understand the truth and will present it in whatever form they wish. They have to renounce the noxious notion that the public's resentment is a measure of the press's virtue, that being loathed means you are doing a good job. On the contrary, if the press is loathed, it will be abandoned as viable competitors arise.

Like it or not, journalism is now in partnership with the public. Reporters will have to learn how to listen. It's not so bad, after you do it awhile.

■ Be gatekeepers. Your job in the new world remains critically important. Most Americans acknowledge that they are overwhelmed by information and technology; they very much need, want and will pay for sanity and coherence.

We can't keep up with all of the books, magazines, cable channels, Web sites, and online conferences aimed at us. We need a clearinghouse, an institution to help sort through everything, to be brave enough to tell us what we need to pay attention to and what's expendable, to offer opinions and help us shape our own. "Objective," passive media are useless in this regard, giving us stalemated versions of truth from the usual suspects but little help in evaluating them. And they're increasingly alien to new generations of consumers used to expressing themselves freely and interactively. What we need are well-informed Sherpas who will cut through the gobbledygook and tell us the truth as they see it, with enough solid, reliable information so that we can make up our own minds.

■ Stand for something. The heart of media is morality, as Thomas Paine understood. Here and there, we hear echoes of the morality that made his essays bristle with outrage and crackle with clarity. Edward Murrow wasn't a particularly brilliant reporter, but he had a moral passion that made an entire industry respectable. Walter Cronkite's force came not from his interviewing skills, which were mediocre at best, but from his occasional willingness to step out from behind the journalistic mask, as when he turned on the Vietnam War or shared his joy and wonder at space exploration.

Modern media, owned by corporations whose only obligations are to stockholders and whose only ideology stems from balance sheets, have lost their fervor. Given the stifling notions of balance and objectivity, they've come to value amorality. The digital culture, on the other hand, is powered by a powerful sense of moral purpose—information wants to be free, individuals have the right to express themselves. Such ideas aren't always practical, but they're inspiring, nonetheless.

Modern journalism has drifted into all sorts of ethical and moral quagmires. Consider the big fees that some of the most prominent members of the bloated Washington press corps take from institutions and lobbies that they cover. Consider the reporters scrambling to cash in on book and movie deals sparked by the stories they cover. Or the parties that magazine editors in New York give and are given, with celebrity guests arriving in limousines. Journalists have lost their sense of outsiderness, the detachment from power that was at the heart of the moral power that fueled the press for years.

You need to care about something beyond obtaining quotes from people on all sides of every issue. You need to tell us what you care about and why. You need to care less about getting the right table at lunch.

■ You're not cops, judges or priests.

The press as an institution seems oblivious to the hypocrisy and resentment it engenders by intruding into the private and sexual lives of others while consistently refusing to put its own members under similar scrutiny.

Journalists may be the people in public life least equipped to grapple with judgments about good and evil, questions that are more logically the province of philosophers and theologians. The idea that a political reporter should decide if a candidate's private relationships disqualify him or her for public office is far from the vision that any founder of the nation or the press ever had.

Can a senator be unfaithful to his or her spouse and still introduce important legislation? Can a president have multiple sex partners and still ease the federal deficit? Was Gary Hart unfit for the presidency because he had a photographed affair with Donna Rice? Was the resulting election of Ronald Reagan better for women than a Hart presidency would have been? Has the Gennifer Flowers affair had any remote bearing on the Clinton presidency? Do any of us yet understand whether Whitewater merits a fraction of the time and effort that have gone into investigating it?

Journalism has failed to resolve any of these moral conundrums, yet it arrogantly injects itself into the heart of the political process, harassing candidates, driving some out of public life, keeping who knows how many others from running. This is an enormous power snatch by a press reaching for a role nobody ever meant it to assume. And this at a point when public confidence in journalism is already at an all-time low.

The mandarins who run the press should bring these creepy character inquisitions to a halt. Those who want to pursue this brand of investigation should sign on with the FBI and get badges and guns. Morality in media comes from fair-mindedness, love of facts, passion for truth-telling and hell-raising—not from airing individuals' extramarital affairs. If journalism doesn't rediscover a genuine sense of moral purpose—one that inspires, not enrages, the public—it will lose even more ground to new media.

■ Raise some dust. Have some impact.

Modern journalism seems to be content with declaring itself more serious and substantive than its competitors, but when you try to think of the last really substantive thing you read or saw, the conceit wears thin. Journalism could do us and itself some good if it stopped judging people's character and unleashed its reporters to take on the really tough issues—poverty, race, violence, welfare, education.

But how much serious journalism is actually being produced these days? Investigative reporting, something journalism is uniquely qualified to do, has become almost extinct at newspapers and network television. Instead, we are barraged with make-believe investigative reporting: How safe is your lightbulb? Is that telemarketer really telling you the truth about where your charity donation goes? Meanwhile, why didn't any of those hundreds of Washington reporters know what Oliver North was up to in the basement of the White House? Why didn't big-city newspapers consider the devastating consequences of the deinstitutionalization of the mentally ill until suddenly the streets were awash with the homeless?

Journalism should be raising hell on our behalf, not by peeking into candidates' bedrooms but by digging deeply into government waste, evaluating the utility of social programs competing for fewer and fewer dollars, offering provocative and aggressive coverage of racial tensions, between riots as well as in their aftermath.

Want our attention? Do something that compels it.

■ Value creativity. Almost every other medium is more creative at the moment than the mainstream press, from the irony of Dr. Katz (he's no relation) and the bite of *Politically Correct* on Comedy Central to the compelling dramas retaking prime-time TV to the brilliant voices emerging on the World Wide Web. Meanwhile, journalism clings to the notion that the new media are a fad, that the young will come to their senses and return.

At the turn of the century, pioneer journalists like Lincoln Steffens and Nellie Bly invigorated journalism with muckraking reporting about brutal social conditions and political corruption. William Randolph Hearst's tabloids inflamed public opinion but also engaged it. In the sixties "new" journalists like Tom Wolfe and Jimmy Breslin brought unusually vivid writing to urban journalism and sparked a whole new wave of nonfiction.

What creative initiatives are under way in journalism today? Network newscasts look almost exactly as they did decades ago, with overpaid anchors in suits reading introductions to other people's stories. Newspapers look remarkably the way they did after World War II. *The New York Times* has yet to introduce color photographs in its news sections, although it's had the technology to do so for years. Cultural coverage remains largely relegated to the back of the book. Many of the most talented and original writers long ago abandoned mainstream journalism for books, film and magazines, which pay better and are often more vigorous. The few new ideas that do surface in journalism—*USA Today,* for example—are ridiculed and derided by the journalistic establishment.

Along with stronger moral underpinnings, journalism is in desperate need of creative transfusions. Without them—without new definitions of news, new approaches to writing, a new commitment to graphics and design, a new moral vision—the media that have shaped our century will wither.

Don't let that happen, not without a fight.

Chapter 10

THE SENSIBLE PERSON

Politicians have been exploiting fears about culture forever. Senator Estes Kefauver did it in the fifties by holding hearings on Wonder Woman and Batman and Robin, a move that led to a self-censoring code adopted by the comics industry. Dan Quayle took on single mother Murphy Brown. Pat Buchanan caws constantly about "the cultural war going on for the soul of the country." Bob Dole tried to make cultural values the heart of his presidential campaign. Newspaper columnists and editorial writers have joined in. Boomer parents, desperate to create brilliant, competitive, "cultured" children, reject many other messages from conservatives like Quayle and Buchanan, but they're enthusiastic about this one.

So the notion that we have two distinct cultural choices has become widely accepted. If you are civilized and literate, you stand for thick biographies, sonatas, oil paintings. Otherwise, you watch *Ren and Stimpy,* listen to degenerate hip-hop, zombie out on MTV videos, or disconnect from the human race with your computer, gradually losing the art of coherent writing or speech.

From any distance, the construct of two such narrow choices seems pointless. Why should media and culture be defined by opportunistic politicians and out-of-touch journalists? Why can't we each make sensible choices that draw from different elements of media and culture, choices that challenge and educate our kids, that fit into our lives?

We can, of course. Sanity begins by ignoring politicians and journalists and relying on individual common sense. Enlightened people will educate themselves about media and culture. They will figure out what they need, drawing from some old and some new sources of news, some old and some new culture, some nearly antiquated technology and some glitzy stuff. Bible-waving conservatives, boomer parents, Chicken Little reporters, censors and intellectuals do not have useful answers for us. Their definitions of decency and culture don't work anymore. Since they cannot guide us, we have to make our own way.

The Sensible Person will recognize that different media make sense at different stages of life. For the very young, for example, home entertainment systems incorporating computer games and CD-ROMs are perfect educational, creative and social tools. Parents have the right—the obligation—to screen this new medium early on and decide how their children can use it.

Some games, for example, are racist, sexist and brutal; parents can make it clear from the outset that they won't buy them or allow them to be played in their homes. Other games—MYST, Civilization, the Sim City series—are extraordinarily educational. They require complex planning and reward patience and strategic thinking. They are best played cooperatively, in groups.

Online computer services offer games, reference databases, and other opportunities for children to learn about the world. Some parents ask their kids to check the daily weather forecasts, since government satellite maps of storm systems and other weather patterns are downloaded daily on accessible, easy-to-use systems like America Online's Weather Conference. Tasks like that not only familiarize kids with computers but guide them toward the educational end of the digital culture. Parents can take their kids on Web tours of the world's museums, whose best artworks are available via linked computer sites. They can steer them toward conferences for kids so that children can connect with their peers from all over the world.

Initially, the Sensible Person will sit with her kids, teaching them not to give their phone numbers and addresses out, explaining that they should come to their parents if they encounter anything disturbing online. The Sensible Person may even block services or conferences she finds inappropriate for young children. The Sensible Person knows that computer use requires and develops typing, language and reading skills. In fact, kids' stories on CD-ROM are often easier and more fun for kids to read than books, since they are presented in interactive forms, so that kids can control the pace and imagery.

As kids get older, the Sensible Person can progressively withdraw, understanding that adolescents will be drawn to rebellious, probably offensive, distinctly individualistic forms of culture online, on cable, or in other new media forms. By this time the kids will also be researching school projects online, critiquing movies and TV shows on bulletin boards, connecting with like-minded pockets of culture. At times, they may be exposed to pornographic imagery or language. Taught properly they—and their sensible parents—will deal with it. If sensible people keep a perspective, the Buchanans and Bennetts of the world might actually have to do something about real social problems, rather than playing to phobias about imagined ones.

Young adults will access sophisticated cultural sites on the Net. To browse the Web effectively, you almost have to be a college student, or unemployed; nobody else has the time. As they enter the workforce they will turn to other more specialized media—cable broadcasts, Web sites, online services, professional journals and trade magazines, books.

But then, any Sensible Person continually alters his media choices as he moves through life. The sensible adult will no doubt continue to read books, which after all are portable, can sustain coffee stains and other damage, can be read over days or weeks, can be propped up on the reader's stomach in bed or toted easily onto airplanes, and make sense on windswept beaches.

The Sensible Person will also continue to go to movies, even though films are available on PCTVs and other at-home media. Leaving the house and going to a movie theater isn't simply media consumption; it's a social and often a familial experience. But, of course, the sensible adult will also have a computer, modem and keyboard. He or she will use e-mail, a remarkably efficient, fast and useful means of communication. He can send business messages, stay in touch with old friends, communicate with children at college, join one of the communities entrenched on the Net.

The sensible adult will subscribe to flexible news services—cable for breaking news, magazines for analysis and weekly summaries. If newspapers ever decide to respond creatively to the information revolution, people will subscribe to them. But they will expect interactivity and be attracted to media that offer some.

The Sensible Person will increasingly turn to the Internet for specialized kinds of political information. Native Americans have linked up all over the country, for example. "The Net is a tool that will allow us to forge bonds between the Indian nations. The only thing we have now is the powwow circuit," says one Native American leader. Veterans have also used the Net in this way, along with evangelists, gay teenagers, environmentalists, and members of individual religious communities. The elderly are already pouring online as a means of connecting with others who share their concerns about staying healthy and active, about forming communities when mobility is difficult, about dealing with approaching death.

Online services offer new ways for political organizations to rally the like-minded, alert them to pending legislation, formulate strategy.

Through all the changes, his own and the world's, the Sensible Person will not buy Luddite notions that new technology is destroying civilization and turning us into ignorant zombies. Nor will he accept the idea, pervasive in the digital culture, that computer users represent some kind of master race. There is no reason to make such simple-minded and divisive choices. Each culture complements the other. Taken together, old and new media offer information, entertainment, community-building, civilization.

Chapter 11

THE RIGHTS OF CHILDREN

Children are at the epicenter of the information revolution, ground zero of the digital world. They helped build it, they understand it as well as, or better than, anyone else. Not only is this new machinery making the young more sophisticated, altering their ideas of what culture and literacy are, it is transforming them—connecting them to one another, providing them with a new sense of political self.

Children in the digital age are neither unseen nor unheard. In fact, they see and hear more than children ever have. They occupy a new kind of cultural space. They're citizens of a new order.

After centuries of regulation, sometimes benign, sometimes not, kids are moving out from under our pious control, finding one another via the great hive that is the Net. As digital communications flash through the most heavily fortified borders and ricochet around the world independent of government and censors, children can for the first time reach past the suffocating boundaries of social convention, past their elders' rigid notions of what is good for them.

In many ways, fears for children are more understandable than fears for other groups, and the decisions made on their behalf are more complex. Since they can't always articulate their own values and feelings, it is often harder for adults to know how able kids are to take responsibility, and when to offer it to them. They are obviously more vulnerable. Parents, teachers, even well-meaning politicians, feel an obligation to protect them from perils they are presumed unable to understand or ward off.

Yet many of these fears seem misplaced, exaggerated, invoked by adults mostly to regain control of a society changing faster than their ability to comprehend it.

The idea that children are moving beyond our absolute control may be the bitterest pill for parents to swallow in the digital era. The need to instruct and protect children is reflexive, visceral, instinctive. All the harder then, to change.

THE HEARTS AND MINDS OF CHILDREN

While it seems logical that limitless exposure to violence or sexual imagery isn't healthy, few serious students of child psychology think culture shapes the moral sense of children.

For a century, the study of the creation of conscience was chiefly the province of Freudians, who theorized that every boy lusts after his mother and, as a consequence, sees his father as a powerful rival. Because he cannot have his mother or overcome his father, he represses his erotic love for the former and his anger at the latter. These feelings are replaced by a set of rules—the superego—that control the child's impulses. This process is the beginning, Freudians argued, of the formation of human conscience.

Over time, Professor James Q. Wilson of UCLA writes in *The Moral Sense,* these Freudian notions have become less plausible. Modern studies suggest that conscience—sympathy, fairness, self-control—is formed not primarily by repressed lust and rage but by the innate human desire for attachment. People with the strongest consciences, Wilson writes, are those with the most powerfully developed sense of affiliation. When we disappoint others by acting immorally, we feel shame; when we disappoint ourselves by failing to honor an obligation, we feel guilt.

Conscience is a conditioned reflex, psychological researcher Hans J. Eysenck believes. Like Pavlov's salivating dogs, people develop automatic, unthinking reactions. Punished consistently by a beloved parent for telling a lie or stealing a cookie, we become nervous when lying or stealing, even if there is no chance of being caught.

So if parents teach morals, live moral lives, discourage and punish immoral behavior and treat their children in a moral way, the children are much more likely to act morally as adults. If children are left to fend for themselves, are given no such encouragement, they may grow up without a strong moral sense. A child watches the moral judgments and decisions of his parents, his siblings and his peers, and factors in the degree of rationality and respect with which he is treated, in forming his own value system.

The idea that a TV show or a song lyric can transform a healthy, connected, grounded child into a dangerous monster is absurd, an irrational affront not only to science but to common sense, to what we know about the children in our lives. It is primarily the invention of politicians (who use it to frighten or rally supporters), of enduringly powerful religious groups (which can't teach the young doctrine and dogma without control), and of traditional journalism (which sees new media and new culture as menaces to its own once-powerful and highly profitable position in American society).

We have reason to worry about violence: Americans kill one another eight times as often as citizens of other industrialized countries. Notice, however, how the media make little distinction between underclass and middle-class problems. Consequently, parents who complain that culture is dangerous seem not to grasp that middle-class children are pretty safe and usually enter the mainstream of American life and opportunity.

David Berliner (an Arizona State psychology and education professor) and Bruce J. Biddle (director of the Center for Research in Social Behavior of the University of Missouri) point out in *The Manufactured Crisis: Myths, Fraud and the Attack on America's Public Schools,* that nationally, 90 percent of students say they felt "very safe" or "somewhat safe" in their schools. Nearly three-quarters say they live in neighborhoods with "hardly any" crime or "none at all."

V-chips and other blocking software will not help the children, mostly from the underclass, who are suffering from epidemic violence. Nor will they make already safe middle-class children any safer. They simply help us to buy into the great lie that violence comes from culture rather than from endemic racial, social and economic problems. It suggests that we are helping children at risk when we are, in fact, abandoning them to their fate.

As for the idea that children are being made dumber than their elders, what most research shows, again, is that well-tended, well-off American children do well academically, while the abandoned and impoverished struggle. Not much news there. The odds of academic achievement and economic success have little relationship, one way or the other, to cultural preferences.

In fact, though Americans are always telling pollsters they fear for their children's brain cells amid the perils of TV and computers, in August 1995 college-bound seniors earned their best cumulative scores since the early 1970s on the Scholastic Assessment Test, making most of their long-term gains in math. "This is the best-prepared class in recent memory," said Donald M. Stewart, president of the College Board.

Test scores like these—far less prominently reported than studies showing that kids don't know who Harry Truman was—make no sense in the context of the mediaphobic concerns about children and culture. How could students boost their SAT scores so dramatically when they were buying gangsta rap CDs, watching vulgar TV talk shows, surfing the Net and watching cable in record numbers?

Berliner and Biddle even question the conviction that American public school students are losing ground intellectually. Responding to the intensifying attacks, Berliner and Biddle decided to learn why so many politicians were scapegoating public education for the nation's social problems.

"Some of those who have accepted hostile myths about education have been genuinely worried about our schools, some have misunderstood evidence, some have been duped, and some have had other understandable reasons for their actions," they concluded. "But many of the myths seem also to have been told by powerful people who—despite their protestations—were pursuing a political agenda designed to weaken the nation's public schools, redistribute support for those schools so that privileged students are favored over needy students, or even abolish those schools altogether."

Typical of the media's dim view of our educational system was a 1995 survey by the Pew Research Center (formerly the Times Mirror Center) for the People and the Press. On average, said the report, only 20 percent of respondents aged eighteen to twenty-nine paid close attention to the kinds of stories listed in the Center's "News Interest Index," which included business and financial news, legal stories, international policy/politics, domestic policy, sports, crime and science. (Interestingly, the young paid less interest to "celebrity and scandal"—only 13 to 15 percent followed those stories closely—than to any other category of news).

What surveys like this, which shape both journalism and public perception, really demonstrate is that the interests of the young are different from those of their parents, and that traditional journalism doesn't address them. Having different cultural and social interests from one's parents' isn't quite the same as being stupid, although journalists seem to think it is.

WHEN I WAS A KID

So much was expected of the boomers. They went off to college in record numbers. They helped stop the Vietnam War and bring down a dangerous president. They talked much about Revolution, embracing radical new music, defying their parents, making popular culture a national religion, raising hell about racism and poverty and a degraded environment.

It seems that most of their dreams and ambitions collapsed somewhere between the Reagan era and the digital revolution. A dispirited group, they're presiding over a legacy of poverty, homelessness, corporate downsizing, and debased politics, among other sad outcomes.

But there are about sixty-nine million of them alive, according to demographers, and they continue to exert great influence in one sphere, at least—as parents, they are shaping the conflict over children and culture. "As Boomers have charted their life's voyage," write William Straus and Neil Howe in *Generations*, an exploration of American social history, "they have metamorphosed from Beaver Cleaver to hippie to braneater to yuppie to what some are calling 'Neo-Puritan' in a manner quite unlike what anyone, themselves included, ever expected."

The boomers aren't true Puritans, of course. They aren't committed enough. The original Puritans are remembered for their sacrifice, brutality and joylessness. But there are striking similarities. The boomers' parental ideology embraces simplistic notions of good and evil. It is censorious, increasingly disapproving, turning more and more to banning and blocking. It posits narrow definitions of what virtue is. And it is doomed, no more effective at stemming the great tidal waves of pop and technoculture than Cotton Mather was at banishing dancing, profanity, frivolity on the Sabbath and general godlessness.

From the end of World War II onward, say Straus and Howe, whatever space the boomers have occupied has been the cultural and spiritual focus for American society. This, of course, is no longer true. New technologies and social change emanating mostly from the digital world are red hot, the new political and cultural focal points, leaving many boomers glowering from the sidelines. They don't seem to like watching other people's revolutions.

Even though the boomers have seen many of their hopes—for benign government, racial equality, economic opportunity—collapse, they do seem intent on offering their children lives of unending enrichment, as if, having been unable to make the world as good a place as they intended, they have made their children the last repositories of their idealism and aspirations. As if their children's perfection can somehow serve as an antidote to their own disenchantment.

Of course, many boomers were bitterly at odds with their own parents. The men and women who fought World War II had no use for rock and roll, hippies or political radicalism. The boomers are determined to be closer to their children. But as they become the untrustworthy over-thirties, the reactionary parental impulse to condemn whatever is new or different as tasteless and inferior has simply mutated into new forms. As it has a habit of doing, history repeats itself. The kids have again gone to war with their parents, and the parents have about as much chance of winning this round as their parents did the last.

There's a lot to fight about.

The evidence suggests that the young are different from, not inferior to, their elders. Surveys by Peter Hart, Yankelovich and Simmons Market Research have exhaustively documented growing differences in the way the old and young gather information. The young love cable and online communications, for example, appreciating their diversity and outspokenness. They don't take culture as literally as journalists do, grasping that art forms like rap can be hyperbolic, shocking, exaggerated. They inform themselves interactively rather than passively. They like media that take themselves less seriously than *The New York Times* or CBS News; they are allergic to men in suits telling them what to think.

As *American Demographics* has reported, young adults are also more liberal than their elders, including the self-admiring boomers. And they are more generous: 49 percent of those age eighteen to twenty-four "approve of giving preferential treatment to minorities to improve their situation," compared with only about one in three boomers.

Maybe the thing that would most help the country's civic life would be for the young to start teaching moral values to their parents.

JOHN LOCKE AND THE SOCIAL CONTRACT

John Locke, the seventeenth-century English philosopher and essayist, was, along with Paine and Jefferson, a pioneer architect of modern democracy. The son of a prosperous Puritan lawyer, he wrote extensively about government and psychology but is perhaps most remembered for his political philosophy. Locke introduced what was at the time a jarring idea: that people should have some say in the way they were governed.

Locke preached that people naturally possess certain rights—life, liberty and property. Rulers, he wrote, derive their power only from the consent of those people they rule. Government, then, is essentially a social contract: subjects give up certain of their rights and submit to the authority of government and laws in return for just rule and the safeguarding of what is rightfully theirs; the ruler holds his power only so long as he uses it justly. If that sounds familiar, it's because Locke's intellectual fingerprints are all over the Declaration of Independence and the Constitution; he was a primary influence on the leaders of the American Revolution.

Under Locke's contract, if the government violates the trust placed in it by the people, if legislators "endeavor to take away and destroy the power of the people, or to reduce them to slavery under power," then government forfeits the authority the people have given it. The contract requires mutual responsibility, and an arbitrary or destructive ruler who does not respect his subjects' rights is "justly to be esteemed the common enemy and pest of mankind, and is to be treated accordingly." Locke was always vague about just what "accordingly" meant, but at the very least, he suggested, subjects have the right to protest and challenge authority when the social contract is breached.

The idea of a social contract emphasizing mutual responsibility rather than arbitrary power seems especially relevant to the rights of children and the extent of parental authority, as the cultural battles rage in America's households and its political arenas.

There are frequent discussions of children in Locke's writings. He strongly challenged the belief, widespread then and now, that the power of parents over children is "absolute," like the power of monarchs over their subjects.

Locke believed the real source of parental authority was moral clarity, trust and rationality. He believed in the moral education of children, rather than the arbitrary imposition of rules. Children, like adults, were entitled to a measure of freedom that was appropriate to their status in the world as rational human beings.

"Parental power," he wrote, "is nothing but that, which Parents have over their Children, to govern them for the children's good, till they come to the use of Reason, or a state of Knowledge, wherein they may be supposed capable to understand that Rule, whether it be the Law of Nature, or the municipal Law of their Country they are to govern themselves by."

The young will probably never have their right to culture and information legally spelled out or enforced. And nobody wants a government—particularly one that can't cope effectively with social problems or environmental concerns—to take on family life as well. Besides, the lives of children are far too complex to generalize about. Degrees of maturity, emotional stability, rates of development and learning, and the patience, thoughtfulness and resources of parents, vary too widely to set forth rules. Five-year-olds aren't like fifteen-year-olds. And when it comes to culture, at least, boys are often not like girls.

But that's why the notion that all children—good or bad, mature or not—have some rights in the digital age is so critical. Their choices ought not to be left completely to the often ignorant whims and fancies of individual educators, religious leaders or parents, any more than people ought to be subject to the total control of kings. Parents who thoughtlessly ban access to online culture or lyrics they don't like or understand, or who exaggerate and distort the dangers of violent and pornographic imagery, are acting out of arrogance, imposing brute authority. They endanger their own future relationships with their children, since they will surely be resented. Rather than preparing their children for the world they'll have to live in, they insist on preparing them for a world that no longer exists. Such parents are to be esteemed the common enemy and pest of children.

The young have a moral right of access to the machinery and content of media and culture. Culture is their universal language. Media are their means of attaining modern literacy, which in the next millennium will surely be defined as the ability to access information more than to list the presidents. Media savvy may mean the difference between economic well-being and opportunity and economic barriers and hardship.

Kids should not have to battle for the right to watch MTV, particularly if they have been given the chance to develop a moral and responsible ethic and are willing—as in Locke's notion of the social contract—to meet their responsibilities.

THE RESPONSIBLE CHILD

The big difference between children and other groups that seek political equity is obvious: some children *can't* take care of themselves. Some are too young; others are physically or emotionally unable; most are not trained to make rational decisions about their own lives.

It is impossible for our legal system to cover the culture disputes between children and their families. No one can spell out every circumstance in which a child is or isn't ready and entitled to assume more responsibility for his or her decisions. And wildly varying family values make it difficult to codify universal rights.

But start with the notion of the Responsible Child. He or she is a teenager, or close to it. She meets these criteria:

■ She works to the best of her ability in school. She may not be a straight-A student, but she's engaged with, and reasonably responsible about, her education and functions successfully in a classroom.

■ She carries her weight at home. She does the tasks and chores she has agreed on or been assigned to do. She doesn't have to do them cheerfully.

■ She's socially responsible. She avoids drug and alcohol abuse and understands that smoking is dumb. She doesn't have to be angelic.

■ She does not harass, steal from or otherwise harm other people—siblings, friends, fellow students— though she will screw up from time to time.

The Responsible Child is not the embodiment of some utopian vision; she can at times be difficult, rebellious, obnoxious, moody. But the Responsible Child makes a good-faith effort to resolve differences verbally and rationally. Saintliness is not required.

The vast literature on children and child psychology contains arguments about almost every conceivable child-rearing issue. But respected experts conclude nearly unanimously that dominant character traits don't magically appear during the teen years. They get formed much earlier, in the interaction, attention and environment provided for small children from infancy.

Advocating children's rights is not synonymous with permissiveness. Scholars of childhood agree that children need clear boundaries, occasional discipline and guidance in shaping their characters. But if children have never had the opportunity to make cogent, informed decisions about themselves—what to eat, when to sleep, what to wear—they can't be expected to suddenly control their cultural lives at age fourteen without help.

By that age, children may already have rejected narrow adult definitions of culture, literacy and education—which tend to involve piano lessons, "serious" books, and proper spelling. They are probably already embracing the rebellious culture described by Alison Lurie: They'd rather be Peter Rabbit than obedient Flopsy or Mopsy. What's changed is that children are now connected, through technology, with one another and with much of the planet beyond. For the first time, they can instantly reach far past their individual experiences. They are much less dependent on parents, siblings, clergy or educators for their perceptions of the world outside their own houses and schools. Using bulletin boards and online archives, autobiographical and linked Web pages—the whole array of new media— middle-class kids now have immediate access to unimaginable resources of their own, the most significant and potentially political of which is one another.

THE RIGHTS OF CHILDREN

The Responsible Child has certain inalienable rights, not conferred at the caprice of arbitrary authority, but recognized by society as inherently belonging to every person.

Children have the right to be respected, to be accorded the same sensitivity that other disenfranchised minorities have grudgingly been granted by the rest of society. They should not be viewed as property, as helpless or incompetent to participate in the decisions affecting their lives.

They should not be called "stupid," not have their culture blamed, without evidence, for "dumbing them down," not be branded ignorant or inadequate because their educational, cultural or social agenda is different from previous generations'. They have the right to help redefine what education, literacy and civic-mindedness are.

Children have the right to communicate with clergy, politicians and educational leaders who claim to know what is best for them.

Children who meet their personal and educational responsibilities ought to have access to their culture, particularly if they demonstrate an ability to regulate their use of it and balance their lives in appropriate ways. They ought to have exposure to the new technology—computers, cable channels and, soon, PCTVs—which allows them to experience culture, information and education.

Children have the right to form like-minded communities through personal Web sites and home pages, on-line services, e-mail, the range of possibilities created by the existence of Net.

Children have a right to have new media and technology included in their school curricula.

Children have a right to challenge the use of blocking software and other technologies like the V-chip which arbitrarily deny them choice, exposure to ideas and freedom of speech.

Children have the right to refuse to be force-fed other generations' values, as in Bennett's expensive moral tales. They have the right to factual information about violence and pornography—to government and academic studies that transcend the shrill debate about "values," tell the truth about the sources of violence and explore just how dangerous pornography is or isn't.

Children ought to share their culture with their parents and to insist that parents view their television programs, go online, play their computer and CD-ROM games with them before condemning their culture and their choices out of ignorance, prejudice or misinformation.

NEGOTIATING THE SOCIAL CONTRACT

So, how would a social contract about media and culture, a truce between adults and children, work?

The social contract envisioned by Locke applies eerily well to kids. A contract by definition is agreed to, not imposed. Its power comes not from arbitrary power but from a moral base, a desire to do the right thing for everyone, to respect and understand all parties' rights and needs. Parents and children would both have to want an agreement that ratifies the children's rights and makes it possible for responsible parents to feel safe about yielding some of their power.

It follows that families with a history of being able to resolve conflicts are good candidates for a formalized agreement. Those plagued by eternal bickering or ruled by arbitrary and unquestioned authority will have trouble sorting out a social contract, at least by themselves.

Under a cultural social contract, families would first recognize that new culture and technology present a different reality, in which traditional ideas about discipline, censorship and control have become insufficient. The members of the family would think through their own notions about children and culture. What kind of a household do they want to live in? How much power and control are the elders willing to cede? A parent would spell out how much TV or online time he or she finds appropriate, and define what else is expected from the child: religious obligations, domestic chores, school performance.

The child would spell out what access to culture he or she wants: which TV shows, which CDs, how much time online. And she has to specify what she's willing to do in exchange. She must also agree to follow rules of cultural safety: not giving out telephone numbers or home addresses to strangers online, telling parents about pornographic contacts, such as files with sexual content. Media access is granted as a right, but subject to some conditions.

It has to be a good-faith contract. Parents who ask too much will lose their moral authority to make an arrangement like this. Kids willing to do too little will jeopardize it as well. The kid has to demonstrate a capacity to be the Responsible Child. Few parents will trust their offspring to uphold their contracts—to turn off the computer after the agreed-upon time, for instance—otherwise. Some parties would probably have to set aside their broken contracts and keep on fighting.

But digital communities could help by setting up counseling and arbitration services to provide advocates for parents and kids, to settle disputes, to distribute sample contracts and sponsor forums and discussions.

If children meet their end of the social contract, parents would concede that they have a moral right to access the TV programs they want, the CDs they want to listen to, the online services they choose and can afford. Families could begin to rely on trust, negotiation, and communication rather than phobias, conflict and suspicion.

If they are economically able to do so, parents would further agree to provide reasonable machinery—computers, cable, new software—that gives their children access to their own culture.

They would not arbitrarily ban cultural offerings like MTV or gangsta rap simply because such things offend them, but would discuss their reservations and objections with their kids. In most cases, the parental objection would give way to the kids' preference, assuming the other conditions are met. This is part of the power these particular rulers would be ceding.

Parents would agree to take political and journalistic hysteria with a grain of salt. To challenge distorted or undocumented assertions about the dangers of new media. To not accept reflexively the idea that violence is caused by pop culture or that the online world is a dangerous, perverted place. They'd agree that definitions of what's "offensive" vary widely—rap might horrify one adult but pass muster as an acceptable form of political and cultural expression to another.

Accordingly, parents won't deride their kids' culture. They'll have to accept that definitions of culture and literacy are changing too rapidly to impose such narrow-minded definitions.

Naturally, if either side violates its agreement—if kids fail in school, refuse to participate in the care of the household, start drinking—all bets are off. But the millions of American kids who can handle a racy chat room or an episode of *NYPD Blue* won't be denied cultural freedom because of their parents' fears about the kids—often very different—who can't.

THE POLITICAL POWER OF CHILDREN

Cultural conservatives, politicians, parents, teachers, adults in general—and especially journalists—have greatly underestimated just how political an issue assaults on kids' culture are.

In topics online, on Web sites, on countless live chats, the young have vented their anger at congressional efforts to legislate "decency" on the Internet and to curb free speech in this freest of environments. They've generated e-mail, bordered Web pages in black, sparked campaigns and protests, letter-writing efforts, even traditional street demos.

This is as intensely aroused and political as kids have been since the seventies. The digital generation has an organizational weapon no previous generation had: the ability to find and talk to distant allies just a modem away. In this way, they measure their own lives against others'; they separate rhetoric from their own experience. They know their culture isn't dangerous. Their connections and alliances, although almost completely out of sight of parents and beyond the consciousness of journalists and politicians, could transform the politics of the young.

Journalists have underreported the extent to which culture *is* politics, to the young; they've underestimated how much the young resent media suggestions that their culture is rendering them stupid, indifferent, violence-prone. Since children are almost without a voice in traditional media or in the political debates on issues affecting them, it's not surprising that their outrage goes largely unnoticed.

But the press is learning the high cost of relentlessly patronizing and offending kids—it has alarmingly few young consumers. Politicians may soon be learning the same lesson. The battles over new media are likely to spark enormous youthful politicization, reminiscent of the movements launched by racial minorities, women and gays.

It won't be that hard to organize. Under the very noses of their guardians, the young are now linked to one another all over the world. They already share their culture online, trading information about new movies and CDs, warning one another about viruses, sharing software and tech tips. At times they band together to chastise or drive out aggressive, obnoxious or irresponsible digital peers. They steer one another to interesting Web sites. And they have developed a fierce proprietary feeling about their online freedom.

Rights have little meaning without some measure of political franchise. Children need concrete political power.

By now, they should have had some help with this. The online culture should perhaps fund a Children's

Digital Freedom Center, similar to the idea behind the Electronic Frontier Foundation (EFF). It could provide children with truthful information about violence, pornography and online safety with which they could educate their classmates and confront ignorance and misinformation about their culture. It could also provide legal support to young people penalized for free expression online or unfairly denied their right of access to culture in school.

THE V-CHIP: DIGITAL PLACEBO

A group calling itself the National Television Violence Study issued yet another "definitive" report in 1996 that concluded that "violence predominates on television, often including large numbers of violent interactions per program." This study, like previous and similar ones, generated substantial publicity and was invoked by members of Congress to justify passage of legislation requiring the V-chip.

Groups of coders, selected from undergraduate volunteers at two participating universities, were asked to watch shows and tabulate violent acts based on the following definition: "any overt depiction of the use of physical force or the credible threat of such force intended to physically harm an animate being or group of beings."

The group conceded that Wile E. Coyote's being pushed off a cliff would probably count as violence in their survey, because "there was intent to commit harm." Presumably, then, millions of parents will use the V-chip to protect their offspring from *Road Runner* cartoons.

At about the same time, *Newsweek* ran a story called "Parental Control Ware," a cheerful consumer guide to blocking software, "the alternative to censoring the Internet." *Newsweek* recommended four programs—Cybersitter, Surfwatch, Net Nanny and Cyber Patrol. The very names are patronizing and demeaning.

One program would automatically block children from a Web site on the poet Anne Sexton because her name includes those three scary letters *s-e-x*.

This approach is the antithesis of trust and rational discourse between adults and children, and more evidence of the growing need to protect children from adult abuses of power.

Blocking software is noxious and potentially unlimited. Once applied, the censoring and restrictions will spread inevitably beyond violence into other areas adults want to place off-limits: political topics that differ from their own values, music and movie forums that don't conform to their adult tastes, online friends they don't approve of.

Although it's being introduced in America as a means of protecting children, this technology, as it evolves, it could easily become the tyrant's best technopal, offering ever more ingenious ways to control speech and thought. Some children reared on this stuff will inevitably grow up thinking the solution to topics we don't like is to remove them from our vision and consciousness. In any other context, defenders of freedom and free speech would be bouncing off walls.

Like the movie industry's silly ratings codes, blocking software gives the illusion of control. It doesn't ensure safety, since sophisticated evildoers will circumvent it even more quickly than kids will. And it doesn't teach citizenship in the digital world.

As parents withdraw, secure in the conviction that their Net Nanny will do the work they should be doing, count on this: Children, many of whom helped build the digital culture, will circumvent this software, and quickly. They would be much better off if their parents accompanied them when they first set out online, showing them what is inappropriate or dangerous.

Blocking deprives children of the opportunity to confront the realities of new culture. Some of it is pornographic, violent, even dangerous. They need to encounter those situations in a rational, supervised way in order to learn how to truly protect themselves.

WHAT CHILDREN NEED IN THE DIGITAL AGE

Children need to get their hands on the new machines. They need equal access to the technology of culture, research and education. Poor and working-class families have few computers compared with the educated, affluent middle class. And we are learning that some minority children are resisting computers as the toys of the white nerd.

But if new technology can create a gap between haves and have-nots, it can also narrow it. Cheap, portable PCTVs with computers and cable modems would equalize access to the digital revolution in a hurry. Making that happen should be the first and most pressing moral issue of the digital generation.

Children also need to learn to use the machinery of culture safely and responsibly. That means grasping the new rules of community in the online world, acquiring digital manners and courtesy, transcending the often abrasive, pointlessly combative, disjointed tone that permeates many online discussions. They need to learn how to research ideas, history and culture as well as to chat and mouth off.

They need to understand from an early age that their culture poses challenges and responsibilities, even some dangers. That time with TV or computers needs to be managed, considered, kept in proportion. That they need to get help if they can't do this themselves. New technology can enhance social skills and broaden experience, but it also raises all sorts of unexplored political and civic issues for the young—how ideas travel and are debated, how the like-minded can link up, how to sort through the growing options.

Children need help in becoming civic-minded citizens of the digital age, figuring out how to use the machinery in the service of some broader social purpose than simply entertainment or technology for its own sake; how to avoid the dangers of elitism and arrogance; how to manage their new ability to connect instantly with other cultures.

But more than anything else, children need to have their culture affirmed. They need their parents, teachers, guardians and leaders to accept that there is a new political reality for children, and the constructs that governed their own lives and culture are no longer the only relevant or useful ones.

They are never going back.

Chapter 12

A FINAL WORD

The media were never meant to be repositories of personal or societal values. They are reflections of them. They serve as the arenas in which we make and shape arguments, pressure our government and hold it accountable, attempt to forge a more just, efficient, educated and humane world. Media don't lead; they follow. They don't create our world; they offer us a picture of it.

The media don't render our culture smart or dumb, civilized or raucous, peaceful or violent. They mirror the state of the existing culture. If you watch TV long enough, on enough different channels, you can see as clear a picture of contemporary America as is available from any distinguished reporter anywhere. The O. J. Simpson trial was not, after all, a mere celebrity scandal but a piercing, bitingly truthful, look deep into the heart of contemporary America's soul—its racial morass, its gender wars, its troubled system of justice.

Media, new or old, don't shape the national character. They don't create the economic, racial, social and ethnic divisions of contemporary America. They don't cause poverty, traffic in guns, induce teenage girls to bear children or teenage boys to abandon them. They don't fund schools or make them ineffective or scandalously bad. They don't shape the consciences or values of children. Despite their many pretensions to the contrary, they don't forge our civic or political consciousness either.

Claims to the contrary are as cruel as they are false—they keep us from seeing and treating the problems we really do face, along with their causes.

The media can't bear all this weight. Values, in the final analysis, seem to arise elsewhere. They come from spiritual, educational, social—and increasingly, virtual—communities.

Values come from leaders, who set (or don't) a tone of truthfulness, compassion and vision.

They come from education, which prepares (or doesn't) children to live and work in the coming world, not in the past.

And most of all, they come from families, where the patience, care, thoughtfulness and rationality of parents shape the consciences of children, provide them with the means of structuring their own values and teach them, through hundreds of daily examples, how we want children and adults to behave.

We have surrendered public discussion of moral values to opportunistic politicians, cultural conservatives, politically correct ideologues and self-righteous jour-nalists. We have succumbed to the continually re-peated notion that our values are being undermined by outside, mostly cultural, forces bombarding us with ugly images, and that if we can just make these power-ful images disappear, our "values" will resurface.

What we seem to have lost in the cultural debates is the sense that values come not from them but from us. We are unwilling to take responsibility for the ethical and moral value systems within our own homes.

Whatever values we have, impart to our children, pursue in our own lives, are reflected in one form or another in the universe of programs, conferences, pub-lications, broadcasts, movies and Web pages we call media. V-chips won't keep us safe. Blocking software won't protect our children. Only we—and they—can do that.

In the end, America's cultural wars are as pointless as they are unwinnable. We have created the richest cultural life in the world. Some of the things our cul-ture creates are garish and awful, some spectacular and brilliant. We get to decide which varieties we use. We get to introduce our children, carefully and thoughtfully, to a world of once-unimaginable variety, creativity and stimulation.

This seems cause for celebration, not alarm.

INDEX

ABOUT THE AUTHOR

JON KATZ is a media critic and novelist. He is contributing editor of *Wired* and has written for *GQ*, *The New York Times*, *Rolling Stone*, *New York* and other magazines. He is a two-time finalist for the National Magazine Award. He was listed as one of the country's most influential media critics in a survey conducted by the Gannett Center's Freedom Forum Foundation in 1995.

He has published five novels. He was formerly executive producer of the *CBS Morning News* and a reporter and editor at *The Washington Post*, *The Boston Globe*, *The Philadelphia Inquirer* and *The Dallas Times-Herald*. He is the author of Media Rant on HotWired's the Netizen.

He lives in New Jersey with his wife and daughter and is at work on his second nonfiction book.

ABOUT THE TYPE

This book was set in Fairfield, the first typeface
from the hand of the distinguished American artist
and engraver Rudolph Ruzicka (1883–1978).
Rudolph Ruzicka was born in Bohemia and came to
America in 1894. He set up his own shop, devoted
to wood engraving and printing, in New York in
1913 after a varied career working as a wood engraver, in photoengraving and banknote printing
plants, and as an art director and freelance artist.
He designed and illustrated many books, and was
the creator of a considerable list of individual
prints—wood engravings, line engravings on cop-
per, and aquatints.